POWER
TO
CHOOSE

POWER TO CHOOSE
TWELVE STEPS TO WHOLENESS

by

Mike O'Neil,
CAODAC, NCAC I

Nancy M. Newbold
Editor

Charles E. Newbold, Jr.
Associate Editor and Recordist

Action Pages
by
Mike O'Neil
Charles E. Newbold, Jr.

Sonlight Publishing, Inc.
4809 Honey Grove Drive
Antioch, Tennessee 37013

Published in Nashville, Tennessee, by Sonlight Publishing, Inc.

Third Printing, April 1998

ISBN 0-9633454-0-0

Library of Congress Number 92-196675

Quotations from the book *Alcoholics Anonymous* are used by permission of Alcoholics Anonymous World Services, Inc.

All scripture quotations are taken from the King James Version of the Bible, with certain words changed to their modern equivalent; for example, "thou" has been changed to "you," and "saith" has been changed to "says."

Printed in the United States of America

CONTENTS

ABOUT THIS BOOK

The teaching portion of this book is an edited transcription of Twelve Step lectures presented at Bethel Chapel in Nashville, Tennessee, from May through July of 1991. The vernacular has been deliberately retained in order to keep the spirit, flow, mood, and character of the presentations.

The unique and helpful features of this book come out of the blood and gut experiences of a recovering alcoholic and drug user who found the key that catapulted him into the "fourth dimension" in the Holy Spirit.

This book touches on many problems in people's lives, but its emphasis deals directly with a means to solve them. It is, therefore, intended to be a straightforward, understandable, and workable solution to the hurts and pains we suffer, and to the hurting we inflict upon others. These solutions are not for the substance abuse addict alone, but are basic principles that enhance recovery from codependency and other compulsive behaviors, such as addictions to sex, food, work, religion, gambling, abusiveness, etc.

These principles also provide an avenue for those who simply want to go on in their spiritual walk with God. Any individual, however healthy they may perceive themselves to be, can benefit from the experience of going through the Twelve Steps, for their ultimate goal is to establish and improve upon a relationship with Jesus Christ.

The procedures recommended in this book are for personal growth and are not intended to be a substitute for professional therapy when such help is necessary.

Scriptures have been taken from the King James Version of the Bible with certain words changed to their modern equivalent; for example, "thou" has been changed to "you," and "saith" has been changed to "says."

Though I had been free from drugs and alcohol for a number of years, I felt stuck in my spiritual life and growth. I was in a Twelve Step group and I was in church, but I was still in bondage and needed help. I became adamant about getting out of that bondage, and it was a very difficult thing for me to find out how. I went to the people who were supposed to know, and they handed me scriptures or spiritual platitudes which didn't work. So I dug deeper to find out what conditions others had met to allow God to bring His experience into their lives.

That led me to working the Twelve Steps with a friend as they had been originally described—just us two guys. During that time I had a spiritual awakening that I had never had before. I began to get victory in life areas that I had never had before. I began to develop a relationship with Jesus Christ that I had never had before. Other people began to see a change in me and they were attracted to that, so I began to share my experience with other people. They, in turn, did the same thing that I had done and they had a similar experience—a freeing up and a breaking of the bondage in their lives, and a new understanding of God and a real relationship with Him.

This book comes out of my desire over the years to share these things more widely. I've wanted to bring the real life, hands-on experience of the gospel of Jesus Christ in the Twelve Steps to people who want it—those in church and out of church, including those in Twelve Step groups. I've wanted to share the insight into these scriptural principles as God has given them to me, and I've prayed that others could experience a deeper walk with Christ through applying His gospel principles contained in the Twelve Steps.

The steps are a workable, digestible method of involving one's self in God's sanctification process. I've attempted to bring these principles forth in a generic way to bring deliverance to people who are still in bondage in major life areas—those who continue to suffer not just from addictions but from guilt, fear, anger, self-deceptions, self-destructive compulsions, obsessions with self, and codependency.

This book contains an outline of my experience in working the Twelve Steps into my life.

May God guide you as you take these steps!

Mike O'Neil

The Twelve Steps of Alcoholics Anonymous

Step One: We admitted we were powerless over alcohol—that our lives had become unmanageable.

Step Two: Came to believe that a Power greater than ourselves could restore us to sanity.

Step Three: We made a decision to turn our will and our lives over to the care of God *as we understood Him.*

Step Four: Made a searching and fearless moral inventory of ourselves.

Step Five: Admitted to God, to ourselves, and to another human being the exact nature of our wrongs.

Step Six: Were entirely ready to have God remove all these defects of character.

Step Seven: Humbly asked Him to remove our shortcomings.

Step Eight: Made a list of all persons we had harmed, and became willing to make amends to them all.

Step Nine: Made direct amends to such people wherever possible, except when to do so would injure them or others.

Step Ten: Continued to take personal inventory and when we were wrong promptly admitted it.

Step Eleven: Sought through prayer and meditation to improve our conscious contact with God *as we understood Him*, praying only for the knowledge of His will for us and the power to carry that out.

Step Twelve: Having had a spiritual awakening as the result of these steps, we tried to carry this message to alcoholics, and to practice these principles in all our affairs.

The Twelve Steps are reprinted and adapted with permission of Alcoholics Anonymous World Services, Inc. Permission to reprint and adapt the Twelve Steps does not mean that A.A. is affiliated with the program outlined in this book. A.A. is a program of recovery from alcoholism. Use of the Twelve Steps in connection with programs and activities which are patterned after A.A., but which address other problems, does not imply otherwise.

For the purposes of this study, two words in the original Twelve Steps have been changed. In Step One, *alcohol* has been changed to read *our human condition*. In Step Twelve, *alcoholics* has been changed to read *others*.

The Twelve Steps

Step One: We admitted we were powerless over our human condition—that our lives had become unmanageable.

"... For the good that I would I do not: but the evil which I would not, that I do." Romans 7:19

Step Two: Came to believe that a Power greater than ourselves could restore us to sanity.

"O wretched man that I am! Who shall deliver me from the body of this death? I thank God through Jesus Christ our Lord." Romans 7:24-25a

Step Three: We made a decision to turn our will and our lives over to the care of God as we understood Him.

"I beseech you therefore, brethren, by the mercies of God, that you present your bodies a living sacrifice, holy, acceptable unto God, which is your reasonable service." Romans 12:1

Step Four: Made a searching and fearless moral inventory of ourselves.

"Let us search and try our ways, and turn again to the Lord." Lamentations 3:40

Step Five: Admitted to God, to ourselves, and to another human being the exact nature of our wrongs.

"Confess your faults one to another, and pray one for another, that you may be healed. The effectual fervent prayer of a righteous man avails much." James 5:16a

Step Six: Were entirely ready to have God remove all these defects of character.

"Humble yourselves in the sight of the Lord, and He shall lift you up." James 4:10

Step Seven: Humbly asked Him to remove our shortcomings.

"Purge me with hyssop, and I shall be clean: wash me, and I shall be whiter than snow." "Create in me a clean heart, O God; and renew a right spirit within me." Psalm 51:7, 10

Step Eight: Made a list of all persons we had harmed and became willing to make amends to them all.

"And as you would that men should do to you, do also to them likewise." Luke 6:31

Step Nine: Made direct amends to such people wherever possible, except when to do so would injure them or others.

"Therefore if you bring your gift to the altar, and there remember that your brother has ought against you; leave there your gift before the altar, and go your way; first be reconciled to your brother, and then come and offer your gift." Matthew 5:23-24

Step Ten: Continued to take personal inventory and when we were wrong promptly admitted it.

"If we confess our sins, he is faithful and just to forgive us our sins, and to cleanse us from all unrighteousness." 1 John 1:9

Step Eleven: Sought through prayer and meditation to improve our conscious contact with God as we understood Him, praying only for the knowledge of His will for us and the power to carry that out.

"Give ear to my words, O Lord, consider my meditation. Hearken unto the voice of my cry, my King, and my God: for unto you will I pray." Psalm 5:1-2

"Show me your way, O Lord; teach me your paths." Psalm 25:4

Step Twelve: Having had a spiritual awakening as the result of these steps, we tried to carry this message to others, and to practice these principles in all our affairs.

"And Jesus came and spoke unto them, saying, 'All power is given unto me in heaven and in earth. Go therefore, and teach all nations, baptizing them in the name of the Father, and of the Son, and of the Holy Ghost: teaching them to observe all things whatsoever I have commanded you: and, lo, I am with you always, even unto the end of the world.'" Matthew 28:18-20

GETTING STARTED

INTRODUCTION

Many Christians are born from above and filled with His Spirit but are still living defeated lives because of the subtleties of codependent relationships and self-destructive behaviors. There is a tremendous amount of denial when it comes to many of these deep-seated hurts, fears, and resentments. Most are still under a powerless law of guilt and shame wherein they struggle to save themselves. Many Christians remain emotionally crippled and mentally tormented with little hope of ever attaining to that promised "peace that passes all understanding."

Silently they cry out with the masses! Is there any hope? Is there any way to put an end to these self-destructive behaviors? Must I always feel this pain, this shame? Is there any way I can shut down these torments in my mind—these obsessions, these hurts, these fears, this anger, this depression? There's got to be a plain-language way to walk in that victory.

The Twelve Steps are not the only way God frees us, but when Jesus Christ is acknowledged as the highest power, they become a sure help along the way. God really is in the process.

These Twelve Steps are not the goal, but a means toward the goal. They are not the power. They are merely a means toward the release of God's power in your life. The goal is to get that promised peace that passes all understanding which can only be found in relationship with Him who is the Prince of peace, Jesus Christ as Lord.

Therefore, these steps are a means whereby your relationship with Jesus Christ is enhanced. In this enhanced relationship, you are better positioned for Christ to make you over in His image.

Taking these steps is a way to "present your bodies a living sacrifice, holy and acceptable unto God, which is your reasonable service." For you are not to be "conformed to this world, but transformed by the renewing of your minds that you might prove what is the good, acceptable, and *perfect will of God*" (Romans 12:1-2).

"For this is *the will of God*: your sanctification" (2 Thessalonians 4:3). Sanctification simply means separation. God wants you to be separated from the sin that entangles you, from the world that seduces you, and from the bondages that torment you. He wants you free of them and He alone has the power to save, deliver, sanctify (separate) you. He wants you separated unto Him.

You will find that there are things within you that are hidden from your sight. The Holy Spirit will use this process to bring them to light in a safe and loving way so that you can deal with them and get rid of them.

With this experience you will come to appreciate the gentleness, the power, the grace, the mercy, and the love of a forgiving, redeeming God.

With this confidence you will give God permission to remove all that excess baggage that you've been carrying around that you thought you needed but was, instead, bogging you down. You will enjoy the removal of all the lies you thought were truths about you; and, in the removal of all these lies, you will automatically become who you are in Christ.

Things in your life will change. For some people the changes are dramatic, for others the changes are small and gradual. Either way, the changes will continue to occur long after you complete the steps.

Charles E. Newbold, Jr.

HOW TO USE THIS BOOK

The intent of this book is to guide you through the Twelve Steps—not to learn about the steps or to find out how they work, but to help you to actually take the steps yourself, one at a time, thoroughly and completely. Each chapter begins with an explanation of the step and is followed by the Action pages which contain an exercise or questions to answer that will lead you through this process.

Weekly

Spend at least one week on each step. Take the step thoroughly, not going on until you are sure you have completed it. God's power is accessed as each step is truly taken, not as we simply go through the motions.

Be prepared to take up to four weeks to complete Steps Four and Five.

Step Eight requires that you make amends to others. You may find that all the amends that you would like to make require more than a week's time. However, willingness is the key. Go on to Step Nine and be ready to make those amends as soon as it is possible.

Groups

Though you can go through the steps alone, I recommend that you meet regularly with at least one other person and go through them together. Meeting with a small, same-sex group is ideal. A partner or group is good because it's hard to be honest with ourselves. We think we have done a thorough job with the step, but we haven't. Having somebody to go through the steps with us keeps us honest and accountable, enables us to get some feedback, and helps us to see ourselves in an objective way.[1]

---

[1]*The Church As a Healing Community: Setting up Shop to Deal with the Pain of Life-Controlling Problems* is a book designed to help leaders set up a support group ministry using *Power to Choose*. This manual contains guides for preparatory meetings, group rules, meeting formats, and more. A thorough description of this manual and how to order it can be found at the back of this book.

Additionally, Steps Three and Seven require that you take the step in prayer with another person. You'll also need someone to take your fifth step with.

Whether you work the steps by yourself or with a small group, you'll still want to find an understanding person to pray with and talk to as you go through the steps. This person may be your "sponsor." For more information on sponsors, see Appendix 1.

If you form a group, keep it small—no more than six persons.

Because of some of the subject matter that will come up and because of group dynamics that may occur, it's important that the group be either all male or all female.

The procedures are simple. Each individual is to read the text, follow the directions in the Action pages, and write daily in a journal. In weekly meetings, (1) pray for God's help, (2) share your responses to the Action pages, and (3) take prayer requests, praying for one another at the end of the meeting and through the week. The steps that call for exceptions to those procedures are noted in the Action pages. Group rules are guided by love, understanding, and courtesy. *Confidentiality is mandatory.* Be supportive, don't give advice, and be good listeners.

The process

Don't be concerned about how God is going to meet your need or how He is going to use this process. He will reveal to you what you need to know when you need to know it.

Once you have learned to take the steps, the process can be applied to any disorder in your life to bring about a life change—a change that addresses the core issues, not just the symptoms.

ADDICTIONS

Addictions are the result of avoiding the pain in our lives by medicating with a substance, activity, or relationship.

We can become addicted to almost anything. The problem with addictions in general is that they dominate our thoughts, feelings, and behaviors. They rob us of our energy, hinder productivity, destroy relationships, and keep us in guilt, shame, fear, and defeat.

Typically, we medicate with any number of the following:

ALCOHOL

CAFFEINE

CARETAKING

THE CHASE

CHILDREN

CHRONIC ILLNESS

CHURCH ACTIVITY

CLEANING

COMPULSIVE LYING

COMPUTERS

CONTROL

CREDIT CARD/BUYING

DRUGS (Mind and mood altering drugs)

EMOTIONAL ABUSE

EXERCISE

FIGHTS

FOOD

GAMBLING

LOVE

MONEY

MUSIC

NICOTINE

PAIN

PHYSICAL ABUSE

PRESCRIPTION MEDICINE

RAGE

READING

RELATIONSHIPS

RELIGION

SEX

SEXUAL ABUSE

SOAP OPERAS/TV

SUGAR/SWEETS

TALKING

TELEPHONE

VIDEO GAMES

WORK

REALITY CHECK: ADDICTIONS

The following questions are designed to help you break through areas of denial in your life. As you read through them, closely monitor your thoughts to see what particular addictive and compulsive behaviors you have that come to your mind. Be willing to admit these to yourself. This can prove to be a major first step in coming to terms with reality in your own life.

Do you hide or secretly destroy the evidence of things relating to a certain behavior?

Are you preoccupied with that behavior? Does it obsess your thoughts?

Does this preoccupation cost you time and energy that should be devoted to other projects?

Do you go to extraordinary lengths plotting to get what you want or to do what you do?

Are you taking increasingly more risks acting out this behavior?

Do you experience a lot of guilt and remorse as the result of this behavior?

Do you get angry at yourself? Do you feel disappointment for not being in control of that behavior?

Do you make yourself promises to quit?

Do you resolve that this is going to be the last time?

Is this behavior causing you or others harm?

Is it affecting your mental, emotional, physical, or spiritual well-being?

Does this behavior hinder your relationship with God?

Does this hinder your performance on the job, in the home as a mate or parent, or elsewhere?

Is this behavior part of a lifelong pattern?

Do you think your life would be better without this behavior?

Do you feel alone and withdrawn as a result of this behavior?

Do you fear rejection from anyone as a result of this behavior?

Do you fear an ultimate consequence as a result of this behavior?

Do you experience mood changes relating to this behavior?

Do you try to convince yourself that the behavior is not a problem, that it is okay?

Do you try to justify your behavior?

Do you blame another for the way you are in this behavior?

Does this behavior cost you money that you later regret spending?

Does this behavior leave you feeling defeated and hopeless?

Does this behavior appear to give you relief or escape from some problem, trouble, or responsibility in your life?

What is that behavior(s)?

REALITY CHECK: CODEPENDENCY

The following questions are designed to help you break through areas of denial in your life regarding codependency. As you read through them, closely monitor your thoughts to see who comes to mind. Be willing to admit these to yourself. This can prove to be a major first step in coming to terms with reality in your own life.

Do you have an overdeveloped sense of responsibility toward another individual?

Is it easier for you to be more concerned for that other person than for your own well-being?

Do you get lost in your involvement with this other person?

Do you often feel a loss of your own identity because of this person?

Is this other person constantly on your mind?

Are you always figuring out ways to please this other person?

Are you losing touch with your own feelings because of this person?

Are you made to feel by this other person that you don't have a right to your own feelings?

Are you afraid to express your true feelings around this person?

Do you feel alone and isolated because of this relationship?

Are you afraid to make other friendships because of this person?

Does this other person's authority intimidate you?

Are you frightened by this person's anger?

Are you frightened by this person's personal criticism?

Does this relationship cause you to be highly critical of yourself?

Do you feel you are not worth being treated nicely by this person?

Do you allow this other person to cause you pain, anger, or resentments?

Do you feel guilty when you stand up for yourself against this person?

Do you do most anything to hold onto this relationship for fear of abandonment?

Do you easily give in to the demand of this other person?

Do you cling to the hope that this person will change and things will be okay?

Have you tried to change or fix this person?

Do you spend most of your emotional energies reacting to this person rather than acting on your own needs and wants?

Have you tried to numb your feelings about this relationship?

Have you attempted unsuccessfully to get out of your relationship with this person?

Are there subtle ways you try to manipulate this other person to try to get your way?

Who is this person?

Who are others?

See Appendix 2 for more information on codependency.

GETTING STARTED - ACTION

A. *Getting Started*

Getting in touch with your feelings and thoughts and learning to identify the nature of your compulsive behaviors are most necessary if this process is to work. "To thine own self be true." Jesus is the Truth, therefore, it is appropriate to pray at this point.

"Father, cause me to know my true feelings and honest thoughts and help me to identify my compulsive behaviors so that I might answer these questions accurately for my own sake as I begin my spiritual journey. I pray this in Jesus' name. Amen."

Now, allow the Holy Spirit to bring to your mind the right answers for these questions. There is a subtle difference between what the Holy Spirit gently brings to mind intuitively and what we try to figure out intellectually. Begin trusting in the power of God to show you these things.

1. What are your fears and anxieties about taking these steps?

2. Why do you think you might need to take these steps?

3. What needs to change in your life?

4. What do you hope to achieve by taking these steps?

5. How might your life be different?

6. Do you think you're ready to let God go to work on you?

7. Do you believe God is able to use these steps to do this needed work in you?

B. *Begin now to write daily entries in a journal:*
Using a spiral notebook or a special journal book, begin to write on a daily basis. After you read each chapter, follow the journal instructions at the end of the Action questions.

It makes no difference what time of the day that you write in your journal, just cover the last twenty-four hours when you do so.

It makes no difference how lengthy your entries are. Just be consistent and faithful to record something. This will help you to focus on the work that is to be done.

Until you have read the Overview, concentrate on the answers to the following questions in your journal:

1. What things have you noticed about your feelings, thoughts, and behaviors as the result of your plans to work the Twelve Steps?

2. In what ways have you discovered God or sensed His presence in your life today?

3. What victories have you had today?

4. What defeats have you had today?

TAKING THE

TWELVE STEPS

OVERVIEW OF THE TWELVE STEPS

In this overview, we will look at where we are, where we hope to go, and the steps necessary to get us there. These are definite steps that need to be taken. They need to be taken in proper sequence, and they all must be taken to complete your spiritual journey through these steps.

We feel some relief after the first three steps and we have a tendency to stop there. Resist this tendency individually and as a group and move on through the steps.

These demons that we deal with do not go away easily, and even if they do go away, they will revisit. They will return and find your house swept clean all right, but still empty. So they go get seven more demons and return, and the condition becomes worse than before.[1]

We cannot turn a lifetime of bad habits around in a few weeks' time. We can turn some things around almost immediately, but we're kidding ourselves if we think we can arrive at our appointed destination in a few weeks.

I've applied this process in my life for many years and each time that I work the steps, I find new things that I need to get rid of and old things that have come back to revisit me.

So, what I want to do in this overview is to give you a picture of what we want to get out of each step, show why each step is important, and how each step leads directly into the next.

Even when you reach Step Twelve, you are not finished with your journey. It is a lifetime process. Step Twelve deals with the sharing of this process with others. God's reason for restoring us is revealed. That reason is to be of maximum service to others. So, let me strongly encourage you to begin at the beginning and stick to it to the finish. This will be the most rewarding experience of your life next to your salvation in the Lord Jesus. This process will touch and alter every aspect of your life—nothing will be left unchanged.

God bless you on your journey.

---

[1]Matthew 12:43-45

The Steps

Step One: We admitted we were powerless over our human condition—that our lives had become unmanageable.

In this step we come to the end of ourselves and find out that we're powerless over a person, a place, a chemical, a habit, a compulsion, or something like that. Eventually we'll learn that we're powerless, period. In our human condition—that is, in our fallen, self-centered nature—we have no power. And this is our dilemma—a lack of power.

Step Two: Came to believe that a power greater than ourselves could restore us to sanity.

We're powerless, and all of us need a power by which we can live, and it has to be a power that has the power to run our lives, and there's only two powers. There's either God's power or the power He allows Satan to have. Everybody serves somebody, and, on a daily basis, you'll either serve God or you'll serve the devil or self.

Also, the wording of the step would indicate that we are insane. You might say, "Well, I may have a couple of problems, but I'm not *insane*. That's pretty strong language. I mean, insane?" For our purposes, insanity is defined as: "Doing the same thing over and over again, expecting a different result—and never getting it." That is, we get the same result which is self-destructive and usually destructive to others.

Step Three: We made a decision to turn our will and our lives over to the care of God as we understood Him.

Having developed some trust in God in taking Step Two, we now let God have these pieces of our lives over which we've been trying, unsuccessfully, to control and exercise our own self-will power.

Step Four: Made a searching and fearless moral inventory of ourselves.

This inventory is an actual writing—picking up paper, writing down and mirroring ourselves on paper as to who we are, what we are, and what we've done. We are looking for patterns in our lives that have been destructive to ourselves or destructive to others.

At this point, the process begins to get tough on us. The first three steps are kind of fun and kind of uplifting, and "oh, boy," and "ain't it neat that God's going to do all these wonderful things for me, and I don't have to do anything for myself like I used to." And then we get into what I call "death valley" which is Steps Four through Nine. This is where the cutting part comes in. This is where we're going to work on getting rid of the things that we aren't, the lies about ourselves, so we can become who we are in Christ.

Step Five: Admitted to God, to ourselves, and to another human being the exact nature of our wrongs.

In this step we share the writing of Step Four with God, ourselves, and another human being. This is a very humbling process, but very necessary if we are to gain the freedom that we seek through these steps.

Step Six: Were entirely ready to have God remove all these defects of character.

Believe it or not, we're going to find one or two defects of character in Four and Five, even though we are perfected in Christ Jesus. Yes, we really are. We become willing to have those removed in Step Six.

Step Seven: Humbly asked God to remove those defects of character.

At this point, we actually get down on our knees and pray a deliberate, specific, and sincere prayer. We begin to release our faith in the ability of God to actually remove those defects of character.

Step Eight: Made a list of all persons we had harmed and became willing to make amends to them all.

Out of what we've done in Steps Four and Five, we're going to have three lists: we're going to have defects, amends, and resentments. We'll need God to help us get rid of our resentments and our defects, and we're going to have to become willing to make our amends.

Step Nine: Made direct amends to those people wherever possible, except when to do so would harm them or others.

In this step we make direct amends to those we've harmed, either by telephone, by letter, or in a face-to-face visit. There are right and wrong ways of taking this step.

Step Ten: Continued to take personal inventory and when we were wrong promptly admitted it.

Step Ten throws us back into Steps Four through Nine. There are three types of inventories in Step Ten: daily, on-going, and periodic.

Step Eleven: Sought through prayer and meditation to continue our conscious contact with God as we understood Him, praying only for the knowledge of His will for us and the power to carry it out.

We continue to grow in our experience and our walk with God through prayer and meditation. Step Eleven is an enormous undertaking as it is designed to implement our walk in Christ in our lives on a daily basis.

Step Twelve: Having had a spiritual awakening as a result of these steps, we tried to carry this message to others, and to practice these principles in all our affairs.

In Step Twelve we're going to give this process or this awakening away to other people. We're going to find that Step Twelve tells us how we'll know when it's timely to give that away and what we're to give away. We'll also look at what it means to practice all these principles in our affairs.

An Outline

Now I want to go over an outline of the Twelve Steps and show you the basic generic goal and underlying theme of the Twelve Steps:

In Steps One, Two, and Three we make peace with God.
In Steps Four, Five, Six, and Seven we make peace with ourselves.
In Steps Eight and Nine we make peace with others.
In Steps Ten and Eleven we maintain the peace.
And in Twelve, we give that peace away.

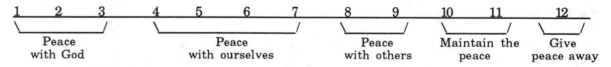

So, as we go through the steps, we make peace with God, make peace with ourselves, and make peace with others. Is there anybody else to be at war with by the time we get past Step Nine? I don't think so. We've covered persons, places, and things.

So *the goal from Step One through Step Nine is to be at peace.*

Peace

What's the big deal about peace? Well, when they were going to take Jesus away, He turned to his guys, and He says, "I'm going to give you a gift."

Just imagine these guys sitting there—they've been stomping the desert for awhile, and they're broke, and their shoes were probably worn out. They've been hanging around with this guy who's been telling them about kingdoms and all this good stuff, so they probably turned to each other and said, "Oh, good! Man, he's finally gonna come across with something."

And He turns to them and He says, "When I leave, I'm going to give you My peace. I'll leave you My peace."[2]

---

[2]John 14:27

Figure what those guys were thinking.

"Peace? What are we going to do with peace? Man, I need two dollars! Give me a new camel—something to eat! Peace? With the Roman army coming over the hill, He's giving us peace? What is this?"

Well, when you think about it, the most sought after commodity on the planet earth is peace. It is peace of mind. They sell it to you all day on television. It's in the beer commercials—go to the lake, go to the ocean—or it's buy this car, eat this, drink that, wear these, get you two or three of those, get a boy, get a girl, two boys, get three girls—everything—that'll make you feel...ahhh, man! Now I'm at peace.

So, it doesn't sound like a big deal until you put it in context with what your insides are crying out for. When I was in my addictions, and even in early recovery, all I wanted was for this brain to just shut up—you know? Just *shut up*!

"What will it take to get this brain to shut up? Am I going to have to go back and drink another quart of vodka and eat some more pills?"

At a time in my addiction that worked. That's why I did it—it worked. That's why I returned to it. It was my best friend. It worked for me. But one day it turned on me and it stopped working.

So, I ended up with an addiction to something that used to be my saving grace but didn't work any more. Now all I had was the addiction. Now I'm just sucking down a case of beer a day and smoking a ton of pot, and I'm just as miserable drunk as I am sober, and the peace won't come. But I can't quit—which finally brings me to the end of myself and makes me willing to quit.

So, the thing that I sought was that peace. And sometimes I'd arrive at it. "Oh, yeah, this is it"...a magic moment. But when it stopped coming, I was lost and addicted. I had to have help to quit.

In Steps One, Two, and Three we make peace with God. That's when we're going to come to terms with our powerlessness, resolve the fact that only God can do for us what we cannot do for ourselves, and allow Him to do it.

In Steps Four, Five, Six, and Seven we do our inventory. That's when we make peace with ourselves. We're going to look at ourselves—this is who I am, what I am. I'm going to embrace this inventory. I'm going to own it. I am the person who does these things—I am this way. I do have resentments. They are not resolved. I do owe amends. Taking the inventory is uncomfortable, but it's liberating on the other side, believe me.

In Steps Eight and Nine, with our list of amends, we're going to make peace with others. We're going to write them letters, call them on the phone, go see them in person. "I owe you an amend." "I harmed you." At this point we will talk about what constitutes harm. And we'll talk about why we go through this process.

Now, in Ten and Eleven, we maintain the peace. There's a formula in here which throws us back into how we got to this point. We're going to be feeling pretty good when we get right here. You can figure on that. If you're at peace with God, yourself, and persons, places, and things, you're not at war. And part of the purpose, and one of the requirements and underlying themes of the Twelve Steps is that *we cease fighting anything or anybody*. We have to.

By the time you get to Step Twelve, you want someone to walk up to you and say, "What happened to you? I want what you have. What is it that you have?"

"Well, I have the peace that Jesus talked about—the peace that passes all understanding, and this is the way I got it. If you'd like to have it, then come with me and do what I did."

So, in Step Twelve, we give the peace away. We're going to give away the whole system, everything we've uncovered about who we are in Christ.

Self-destructive problems

As we do these steps we'll be dealing with any kind of self-destructive problem that stems from dependence on a person, place, or a thing and that causes you to continually end up in some kind of negative experience in life: you're broke—in or out of a relationship—in or out of a job—and so on.

Specifically, we'll be talking about codependency on people, trying to fix people, looking for our own identity in other human beings, workaholism, alcoholism, chemical addiction, people addiction, church addiction, sexual addiction, food addiction, etc. We're going to talk at length about the religious and spiritual abuses that have happened to us and how these have affected our lives.

We're driven people. And there are root causes behind being a driven person. We will look at these—resentments, anger, hurts, pain, low self-esteem and feelings of worthlessness, the past experiences in our life that we're holding on to, grudges, greed, and so on. Those are the things that we're going to find that are driving our bus.

Codependency may be a new term for some of you. It is *"a preoccupation, or extreme dependence on another person or thing,"* but generally on another person. It is an unhealthy dependence—a preoccupation *to the point that you focus so much on that person that you begin to neglect yourself.* Your world revolves around that other person and you even begin to lose touch with your feelings. You can be spiritually, emotionally, mentally, and even sometimes physically dependent. Some people are a little bit codependent; others are extremely codependent.[3]

Power

Power is another underlying theme of the Twelve Steps. If I am powerless to begin with, and I've got to have a power by which I can live, I

---

[3]See Appendix 2: Codependency

also have to have a power by which I can take these Twelve Steps. I guarantee you're not going to take these Twelve Steps in and of and all by yourself in your own strength. You will quit if you try that. You will have to have a power that will take you through. That power will be God.

Denial

Denial is a big issue.

There are two aspects of denial. Initial denial is what most of us have when we hear about the Twelve Steps, or we see this book, or we look at this material and say, "That's a good deal for those people that need that. I'm so glad that somebody came up with a program for those people, and I would like to learn about that program so that if I ever run into anybody that has those problems, I will be able to talk to them about this stuff." That's initial denial.

Secondary denial says, "Well, maybe I'm not perfect. Maybe I do have a defect here and there, but surely I'm not that bad. I'm not *that* bad. I don't have *that*."

It's like a little demon is walking around and somebody taps him on the shoulder and says, "She's trying to figure it out."

"Oh, is she?" So the demon whispers to her, "There's nothing wrong with you. You're okay. They're all jerks." And we buy it.

But as you move through the steps, the denial begins to break open. The process has a way of unearthing it. Our pain is the force that breaks through the wall of denial.

One more thing about that: God will only let you see what you can stand, when you can stand it. That's not denial, that's God. But don't mix the two of them up.

Finally

It's impossible to go through these steps and not be affected—if you go all the way through them. The more you put in it, the more you'll get out of it. The deeper level that you go to, the deeper the experience you'll have.

———— OVERVIEW - ACTION ————

In the overview of the Twelve Steps, you will recall that Steps One through Three have to do with making peace with God, Steps Four through Seven have to do with making peace with yourself, Steps Eight and Nine have to do with making peace with others, Steps Ten and Eleven have to do with maintaining that peace, and Step Twelve has to do with giving that peace away.

Below are a few simple questions that are intended to help you focus further upon peace in your own life. The purpose for taking this action is to create an awareness of those in your life, including yourself, with whom you are not at peace. These questions are not intended to take you beyond that. The Twelve Steps will walk you through that process.

A. *Taking Action*

Prayerfully and honestly answer the following questions:

1. How are you not at peace with God?

2. How are you not at peace with yourself?

3. Who are some others in your life (past or present) with whom you are not at peace? (Include people, institutions, and principles.)

B. *In your journal:*

Continue to make daily entries in your journal. Focus on the information found in the Overview. Answer the following questions each day.

1. What have you noticed about your feelings, thoughts, and behaviors as they relate to the information in the Overview and the Twelve Step process that is beginning?

2. In what ways have you discovered God or sensed His presence in your life today?

3. What victories have you had today?

4. What defeats have you had today?

STEP ONE

**We admitted we were powerless over our human condition—
that our lives had become unmanageable.**

Originally these steps were developed for Alcoholics Anonymous, and Step One said that "we were powerless over alcohol." But because anybody can benefit from these steps, I've changed it to read that "we were powerless over our human condition." It's our human condition that separates us from God and puts some form of idolatrous behavior in place of where God should be. This human condition that all of us suffer is a result of being born of Adam, of coming into this world with that fallen, self-centered, fleshly nature.

I'm going to go backwards through this step. I'm going to talk about unmanageability first, and then powerlessness, and then I'll explain the step.

Unmanageable

We all begin this step at the end and finish at the front. We start with our lives being **"unmanageable."**

The only reason we consider that there's something wrong, or that we need to go talk to somebody, or that we need to take these steps, or talk to the pastor, or anything—is because some area of life, or all areas of our lives, have become unmanageable. It may be over a relationship. It may be over a chemical. It may be food. It could be money. It could be religion. It can be anything or anyone that is driving our bus.

We discover a continuing loop of unmanageability in our lives. It signals us that something is wrong, and we attempt to interrupt it. We *do* go see the pastor, we *do* get out of that relationship and get into another one, or we try to have no relationship at all. We try to stop spending that money.

We try to stop exercising three times a day and running five miles in the morning, at noon, and at night. We try to stop drinking. We try to stop using chemicals. We try to eat moderately and not eat between meals. We try to stop our workaholism. All these things—and more. You fill in the blanks.

We find, however, that whatever it is, we're powerless to stop doing it. We tell ourselves over and over again, "I'm a new creature in Christ.[1] I should be able to do this. Why can't I do this? I must be defective. Something's wrong. I didn't get enough of the Holy Ghost. I've got to go get re-baptized. Maybe when they dunked me, they didn't dunk me deep enough. I need to go get sprinkled, dipped, and dry-cleaned. Something! Next Sunday, I'm going to be down front one more time. Maybe if they hang me upside down and shake me and pray over me, this'll fall out of me." *Any*thing. *Something*.

So we do those things. Some of us will go to counseling. Some of us will change relationships. We'll get married. We'll get divorced. We'll get in a relationship—out of a relationship. We'll quit a job—start a job. Start our own business. Whatever it is. And it doesn't fix it. It just transfers from one obsession to another. We call this "a human doing" versus a "human being."

Dis-ease

Before I talk about what "powerless" means, I want to explain how the natural, fallen human condition is a disease—dis/ease. Out of ease. A dis-ease within myself.

Let's look at this condition and define its parts:

It's a three-fold disease, or dis-ease.

It's physical, mental, and spiritual.

Many of you who have been in Christian teaching have been taught that man is a tri-fold being. This is basically us. This is our makeup.

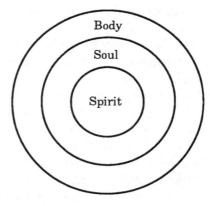

We are a body, soul (or mind), and spirit. That's what we are. We're not one of those things, or two of those things; we're all three of those things all the time until we drop our earth-suit. So this is us moving through our experience in life.

The dis-ease affects the whole man—body, soul, and spirit.

Here are some definitions for these things, and we'll tie those in to what it means in the area of our unmanageability and in our powerlessness.

---

[1] 2 Corinthians 5:17

Body

Physically, we're going to find that there is an allergy of the body.

An allergy of the body for the alcoholic means he can't just have one drink. If he has one drink, he has an allergic reaction and he wants another drink. And he wants another drink. And then when he gets that one, he wants another drink. And another one and another one until he either passes out, falls out, gets knocked out, or whatever.

For those of you who are not alcoholics or drug addicts, let's transfer that definition of allergy over to other things. However you medicate, or whatever your drug or your obsession of choice is, or whatever your addiction that's unmanageable is, it's giving you a mood-altering feeling. It is altering you consciously. It makes you feel good.

"He makes me feel good."

"She makes me feel good."

"Eating three cream pies at two o'clock in the afternoon makes me euphoric."

"Running ten miles in the morning and on my lunch break at work, and working out with weights and then running another ten miles at night makes me feel good. It alters my consciousness."

"Running all over town to spiritual services several times a week where the Holy Ghost is moving, and running down front and getting that buzz and those warm fuzzies makes me feel good ... Now the kids haven't eaten this week, and I've been missing work, but, boy, I'm high on God! Yeah, buddy. Man, God and I—we're groovin'. We are feeling good! One of my kids got arrested last night, but I couldn't be home—haven't been able to be home for the last three months. But God and I are going to take care of it and it's going to be just fine. I'll go get some more warm fuzzies and the kid will get it by association."

It may be money, it may be gambling, it may be spending that money—shopping addictions, people addictions, sports—we can become addicted to anything—whatever it is that alters that consciousness and alters that mood. We can't find significance inside ourselves, so we seek it "out there," and that is the physical addiction of the disease.

Anything and anyplace that we get our significance outside of God is potentially a disease—a dis-ease. It's out of order. It's a lie. It's an imitation. It's a counterfeit. It's a deception. And it's potentially addictive. Because we want to feel that way all the time.

At the time of this writing I've been free from my active addiction for many years, and, I'm telling you, I still want to feel that way all the time. I doubt very seriously if there's any of you who don't want to feel good all the time—if you'll get honest.

The only thing we would rather do than feel good is feel sorry for ourselves. So, it's sort of a contest between "I want to feel really good!" and "Well, I'm not feeling really good, I'm not hittin' that high—so I'll feel sorry for myself. That feels good. I'll wallow in that for a while."

And it feels even better if I can get ol' Joe and two or three other ones to feel sorry for me with me—to get in there with me. They'll say, "Oh, man, that's bad—you should feel *worse* than you feel! I can't *believe* you only feel this bad! You oughta really feel bad about that! ... So, what else is going on? ... they did *what?* Oh, my. Oh, man. I really feel sorry for you."

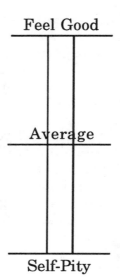

We love it. We love the self-pity. We've got to either be up high or down low. We can't stand it in the middle. Feeling average doesn't do it for us. God forbid that somebody would tell us that we're average! "Do anything to me, God, but don't make me *average!*" Even the word has just a horrible sound to it, you know? Or if we should want to be average, we want to be the most average—the number one average person of the universe.

So, we've got to be number one, either at one end of the spectrum or the other. And whatever we use to get us to either end can become our allergy of the body.

Soul

Obsession of the mind.

I know mentally, as my life becomes unmanageable, that this disease, allergy, addiction, compulsion, or obsession is hurting me—maybe even killing me. "I can't do this any more. This is wrong. I've got to quit." The guy with the weight problem is saying to himself, "I weigh three hundred pounds and I'm still eating cream pies everyday—three of them. I need to stop it."

The mental obsession comes back and says, "Three hundred isn't too bad. Lots of people weigh three hundred pounds. So what if you're only four foot two?" The mental obsession comes back in with rationalization.

The favorite two pastimes of the disease in the mental obsession is **rationalization and self-pity**.

If we're not feeling good, then we are rationalizing—coming up with what we think are good reasons for doing whatever we want to do. We've rationalized how we're going to feel good in the first place. We've rationalized through our mental obsession how we're going to eat our cream pies or drink our scotch or play our sports or go to church six nights a week and neglect the family and the job—or whatever we're going to get our buzz on. We've rationalized getting our feel-goods at whatever expense.

And if we're not feeling good, we're either rationalizing some kind of behavior—or we're feeling sorry for ourselves. For me, the only time this is not going on is when I'm in tune with God—when God and I are in line—and that's usually when I'm praying. So, in essence, if you want to take that a little further, if I'm not praying in some form or another, with an awareness of God's presence in my life, I'm rationalizing, justifying, or feeling sorry for myself.

Denial

The mind is where the battleground is, denial is what's going on, and that's part of the rationalization. We deny, without realizing it, the reality of our situation—and this is where Satan lives.

If I were condemned to hell and had to be a demon, I'd want to be the spirit of denial. He's got the easiest gig of all the demons. He just shoots pool and hangs around.

He hears somebody say, "O'Neil's thinking about quitting drinking." "Oh, he is, is he?"

So, denial tells me, "You don't have a drinking problem. You don't drink any more than the rest of those idiots. *They* are the problem. If other people would get their acts together, you wouldn't have so many problems. So, just have another beer. You deserve a drink. One won't hurt."

And I think, "That's right, that's right. It's them, not me. They're the problem. I need some relief."

And denial goes back and shoots pool. All he's got to do is drop about two dimes on you, and you'll buy it in a heartbeat.

He says, "Eat some more cream pies. I mean they're *good*. And you can handle it. And you're not that bad—three hundred pounds ain't that bad! Some people weigh seven, eight hundred pounds. You got a long way to go."

The drunk tells the drunk, "Man, you still got a job; you still got a wife, a car. You're still functioning. Man, the ones that got problems are down on Broadway or sleeping under a bridge. You don't have a problem. You don't drink any more than *I* do. You're okay."

Denial will also tell you that you're getting away with it. Denial tells you all these things. That's denial and some of the ways that denial works.

Rationalization

These rationalizations are characteristics of the obsession of the mind.

If you're not in God's will and that pipeline to God isn't open, you're off into one of these:

"It's okay for me to do this."

"It's okay for me to have a little of that."

"Gosh, if you had lived my life, you'd be this way, too."

"So-and-so has a new car—I've been doing the same thing he has— why don't I have a new car?"

"I'll get one of these."

"I'll get three of those."

"Your plan for me, God, is not working out as fast as I thought it should." "I'm *so* talented. You made me *soooo* talented. Why don't You do something with all this talent? I've gone here and I've spent lots of time down on music row, skinnin' and grinnin'. Nothing's happening. Maybe I should just go get a lobotomy so that I can't play an instrument at all."

That's still more self-pity, rationalization, and justification.

Worry

Worry is meditating on the lies of the devil. Let me say that again. *Worry is meditating on the lies of the devil.* That's all it is. Worry is *never* godly.

It's another entrance into the area of the soul and the mind and the obsession of the mind to try to attack us and take away our power of choice. As long as we keep the hands of our minds on something, God can't get His hands on it. Somebody said, "If I don't worry, I feel like I'll lose control of what I'm worrying about." That's exactly what needs to happen. We need to let go of what we're worrying about and let God control it.

"Let go and let God." I didn't know what that meant when I first got involved in this program. I'd think, "Let go of what? And let God do what? What are you talking about?" So, I'd just drop everything and stay in bed all day.

But it's letting go the hands of our minds that are on the things that we're obsessing and compulsing or worrying about. If we've got *our* hands on it, how is God going to do anything with it?

The battle

The mental obsession. This is where the attack is. This is where the battle is. Sometimes we're in church and singing about "war in the heavenlies" and all that stuff. I want the one of you who has gotten out of his earth suit, gotten with Michael the archangel, stood next to him, borrowed his sword, gone downtown and whipped some demons—I want to talk to you.

We pray. We do pray. And the war goes on in the heavenlies.

But where does the war go on in me? Right here in my head. This is the battleground. This is *my* war in the heavenlies. And the little spirit guys are warring their heads off in there. And they're doing it through different versions of this mental obsession, trying to activate my dis-ease.

Remember in the overview where we talked about peace? What would dis-ease bring up in your mind? It brings up a lack of peace. Right? If we're at peace, dis-ease ruins our peace. Dis-ease is not peaceful.

Spirit

Spiritually speaking, I'll define the dis-ease as a "blocking of the spirit."

The Bible calls this a hardening of the heart. Through activities, through the obsession of the mind, through guilt, fear, anxiety—we build up a blocking of the spirit man. We block off the Spirit of God. We remove ourselves. We're **powerless over our separation from God**—which is our human condition.

This is where our answer is: in the removal of this blockage of the spirit.

We're going to find as we move through the steps that we get well spiritually first, and then the mental and physical straightens out automatically.

But if we have cut off the Spirit, if we are separated from the Spirit, then we've lost our wholeness.

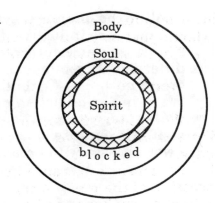

Lots of people call this separation, and validly so, "sin." But I don't want to talk so much about "sin," because sin—and you need know this—sin is a *symptom*. Sin is merely a symptom of the disease. Sin is *not* the problem. It looks like the problem. It acts like the problem. It causes me problems. But it's not the problem.

How many of you have solved sin in a life area, only to have some other thing crop up? It may be something that you didn't even know was a sin—something that's causing your life to become unmanageable, or causing you to self-destruct—or something that's causing you problems in any of your life areas, either spiritually, mentally, or physically.

We chase the symptom. That's another deception.

Now please *don't* hear me say that it's okay to sin. That's not what I'm saying. What I am saying is: **the problem is never the problem—our reaction to the problem is the problem**.

Let me explain it this way: Suppose I'm having *a* drink—it's not a sin to have *a* drink. But it is a sin to get drunk and run over somebody in the car and kill him...or get drunk and get in a blackout and go rob a convenience store. That's a sin. And drunkenness is a sin.

Well, is the problem that I rob liquor stores?

"If we could just get that guy to stop robbing them liquor stores, he'd be fine!"

"Just come on down front here—Lord, deliver this boy from robbin' them liquor stores."

And I come back next week and go, "Yea! I didn't rob any liquor stores. Praise God!" I knocked over a jewelry store down the street, but no liquor stores...embezzled $100,000 over at the job, but no liquor stores.

We haven't addressed the problem. And the problem is the disease. The problem is what's behind the symptom. The problem is our *reaction* to life's problems and how we deal with that reaction.

So, our spirit is blocked, we've got an obsession of the mind, an allergy of the body, and whatever our obsession of choice is—our addiction of choice or whatever's driving our bus and determining our destination. We're just running back and forth between the feel-goods and self-pity. Just back and forth, back and forth, back and forth.

I call it the addiction cycle. It runs in a circle—it just goes around in circles, and we're in it. We do and say all these different things to interrupt it, but it doesn't ever interrupt. It may manifest in a different way—it may look different. It reminds me of an old saying: "It's just the same old whore in a brand new dress"—that's what it is.

We're in the addiction cycle and we're powerless. We've tried all kinds of ways to interrupt it; it doesn't seem to interrupt. The reason we can't interrupt it is because of the blocking of the spirit. We're unable to access the power necessary to break the cycle.

Powerless

Now I want to get to the essence and the heart of the step in terms of being powerless.

I'm powerless because I *can't not* do whatever it is that I'm doing that's killing me or causing my life to be unmanageable. I *can't not* do it. I pray about it. I exercise about it. I do everything that I can do to stop it, and it keeps coming back, and I can't stop doing it.

The essence of the step that I need to take to begin my deliverance is this: I have to admit to myself and to God, "I cannot do this—I am powerless to *not* do this." No matter how guilty I feel about it, no matter what anybody says, "I can't *not* do this."

There's been some spiritual and religious abuse, probably unintentional, by many pastors and teachers. They've said, "You're a new creature in Christ. Just be that new creature in Christ. Quit that! Just stop that! Stop beating that wife! Just quit it! And just get that scripture out and read it: 'I'm a new creature in Christ.' Go home, read that scripture: 'I'm a new creature, I'm a new creature.'" But the guy walks in and...he just smacks her. What happened? He's still trying to do it in his own strength.

Now think about this, and look at the whole picture. If the disease has blocked my wholeness—blocked off my spirit from the Spirit of God—then no matter what I do to fix my problem, it doesn't work because of my source of power. Where am I getting it from? From self. I'm getting it from the soul area (the mind) and the body area (physical). Self.

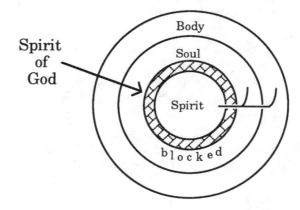

Now what opens up the wall around the spirit? The admission that, in and of myself, I can't stop this behavior or compulsion. Though it seems like a little bitty thing to overcome, I cannot do it.

Admission, willingness, grace

I'm powerless to not do this addiction thing. I need God's help, and I'm willing to let Him help me. "God, I'm willing to drop that ego, drop that pride, drop that self, and let you do whatever You're going to do. And I don't know what You're going to do or how You're going to do it—but I can't quit being the way I am."

That willingness—that admission of *our powerlessness and being willing to let God do for us what we can't do for ourselves—that's what knocks a hole in that wall* around our spirits so that God's *grace* can come in there, open up the spirit, come back out, go into the mind (or the soul) and grab these areas—alcohol, exercise, eating, abuse, any self-destructive patterns. His grace

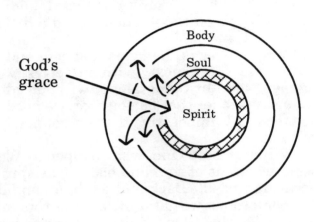

will come in and be sufficient on a daily basis, because we're willing to let Him do this. He will remove the desire and the craving.

"God, remove this desire and this obsession in my mind and this rationalization that goes on everyday to do this and continue in this behavior. *You* remove it. I can't do anything about it except let it go. Take my hands off of it, God."

This is an old saying:

"I cannot think my way out of my problem.

I must act my way out of my problem.

We can't think our way into right living.

We have to act our way into right thinking."

Now, His grace has come into my spirit because *I'm willing* to let it. What a price to pay, huh? And how long do we stay out in the cold because we're unwilling?

Because I'm willing, His Spirit breaks through that wall, flows into me, and His grace does for me what I can't do for myself. Three days from now I don't have a desire to eat a cream pie. Tomorrow I don't want a bottle of beer. "I've gone three days and I haven't smoked a joint. I can't believe it—I haven't even thought about it. How weird. And I didn't do anything. How did that happen?"

The grace of God.

Because I was willing to let it happen. Because I identified my unmanageability and then was able to say truthfully, "God, I've tried for twenty years—I think I'm powerless."

Some of us will say, "There's an outside chance here, God, that I'm powerless. And just in case that's true, I'm willing to let You do it." And He does it. Just like that. That's instantaneous deliverance. Lots of you,

31

maybe all of you, have had instantaneous deliverance in areas of your life. I've just described exactly how it happened.

But sometimes it doesn't happen. The problem is, we didn't give Him *all* of it. We thought He said, "Well, I've got one of these and two of those and three of those ... "

So we say, "Thanks, God—I'll take one of each. That'll do it. I'm handling this other stuff pretty good, and I'll be all right over here. I'll get back with you on this—when I need a little tuneup."

Willingness is the heart and soul and essence of the first step. Without willingness and honesty with ourselves, we can't go on. No matter what baggage we're bringing along, without admitting powerlessness and a willingness to let that baggage go, we need not bother to go on to the rest of the steps. It's imperative that we get a grip on Step One before we move forward.

Without Step One, what happens? We're back in self. We're back in those two areas of soul and body. The spirit is blocked up, so we're operating in self. Back and forth, up and down.

Sometimes we get a little bit of this insight, and we think, "I'm going to do those Twelve Steps, and I'm going to learn all about that, and I'm going to become very intelligent about that, and then I'm going to fix myself— that's what I'm going to do."

So as we move past Step One and Two, and especially after Step Three, there's going to be more and more of a tendency for us to think that *we* are actually making these changes in ourselves. But all we are really doing is fulfilling the conditions that allow God to bring about the changes. "I can't, He can, I think I'll let Him." Remember that. Beware of the tendency of the human condition to get back into self.

This is the way we are: God sends us a blessing of money, and we sit down with a pencil and paper, and we go, "Okay, what did I do? What did *I* do? Let me retrace the last week to see exactly what I did, so I can do that next week, so He'll send me some more money." Blows God's grace totally out of the box. Moves away from our source. Moves away from our healing. Moves away from our God-center into our self-center.

Only two centers to be in, folks. There's only two: God-centered—self-centered. God-centered and self-centered, period. There's no third area and no neutral area.

Powerlessness versus helplessness

Powerlessness over the human condition is not the same thing as helplessness. If I'm powerless, that doesn't mean I'm helpless. But helplessness is a pitfall that the self-pitying, rationalizing, dis-eased person may fall into as he learns about this step.

Helplessness says, "Well, I'm just no good. Can't help myself." And we get into that attitude of self-pity that keeps us in bondage to our addiction. It gives us the excuse to do what we want to do anyway. But powerlessness means I *can't* not do what I'm doing. It's an attitude of reality that causes us to seek a power that can make a difference in our lives. We're burned out with the dis-ease, can't not do it, and don't want to make excuses for it anymore.

Powerlessness versus helplessness. Don't confuse the two in this step.

The power to choose

Now the only power we can have is the power to make choices. The power to choose is the only power God gave us. He created us in His own image and likeness and gave us one thing—a free will, which is our will power, and our will power is the power to choose where we're going to get our power. Until the addiction, the disease, the compulsion robs it from us, we have the power to choose .

That means I have to choose who I'm going to serve. Bob Dylan had a song out years ago called, "You're going to serve somebody." I don't care who you are or what you do, as long as you're in your human suit, everyday you're going to serve somebody. And you'll either serve God or self. The original lie in the Garden of Eden was that "you, Mister Self, can be God." We bought it then, and we still buy it today.

So, the power of choice is what we need to have restored. All addictions and compulsions take away the power to choose. That's where Satan and the demonic realm attack us. That's how he gains victory over us in our lives. If he can remove the only place that I have any power, then he can run my life. And the only place I have power is my free will and my power to choose my power.

One of the reasons that we fall is that we choose *self*-will-power. We're always talking about, "Well, he could stop doing that if he just had more will power." I don't know anybody with more will power than an alcoholic. An alcoholic can get a drink on Sunday morning in the middle of Kansas, in a dry county, and have it delivered to his hotel room when he doesn't have any money and can't get any money. Now, that's *will* power.

Some of you who want to do something, or be with somebody, or go somewhere, or buy something, or operate in whatever obsessive-compulsive behavior you're poison is, you *will* get it done.

So, here's where the deception comes in: if I'm a born-again Christian, and I have some self-will-power, then I'll try to pull myself up by my own bootstraps. Then I fall. We always fall. We cannot do for ourselves what we need to have God do for us. There's two jobs: my job and God's job. I can't do God's job and God won't do my job. My job is to admit that I'm powerless and turn it over to Him.

There's an old saying, "I can't, He can, I think I'll let Him." And that's for everyday. *Every*day. I can't do this. I'm powerless to be doing this lecture except for the power of God.

But don't confuse helplessness with powerlessness. Don't refuse to do this step because you think it insinuates helplessness.

God's power

Think about the step and think about God in terms of power. God is a person. I finally found that out. That only took me thirty-five years. Now that we know He's a person, we need to come to realize that He's got *the* power. All power. We hear all the time about Satan and his power. "Boy, he's got the power to do this and the power to do that." Yeah, Satan's got permission to deceive and accuse and some power if you buy into it. But *God* has *all* the power. Jesus, the person, has *all* the power.

So, I want you to think about this step in regard to God and His power, and in regard to yourself in your powerless human condition and your self-will. When you get into self, then you're serving self and Satan, and that's when he runs your life and when he can take away that power of choice.

Power, control, and authority

Sometimes it seems like we have power because we're able to intimidate or manipulate people into doing what we want them to. But that's not power, that's control.

Sometimes we think we have power because we're the boss, or we're the one in charge of making certain decisions. But that's not power, that's authority.

Real power—the power that we need—is the power to change the nature of a created thing.

To help you know the difference between these three and to understand what you have power over and what you don't have power over, here's a little formula to go by, a rule of thumb.

Power changes; *control* copes; and *authority* rules.

Until we tap into real power, we are powerless to change. In the end, we will find that God alone has the power to truly change things. If any one person or thing seems to have any power to effect change, if it is genuine power, it had to come from God and continues to be the power of God working in and through that person.

Personal experience

I had a high-paying, high-level, high-visibility job until the corporation flew a jet in on a Monday night, pulled me out of it on Tuesday, sat me down, said, "You're fired. Get out. Don't come back. Don't get on the grounds, don't call or visit anybody. Here's your severance pay."

I asked, "What did I do?"

"Nothing, really. We just need to change administrators."

"Oh, really? Okay. Can we talk?"

"No. Bye. Have a nice life. Good luck feeding your family."

I couldn't believe that was the real reason. Just the week before I had been called on the carpet for praying and lifting up the name of Jesus in staff meetings. I was told it showed a sign of weakness on my part. "The big exec doesn't have it enough together, so he has to pray."

I was hurt and I was confused and I was mad. I was real mad—and scared, and all kinds of things. I wanted to know what really happened. Obsessed on it. But I had to get past it. I had to get past it as fast as I could.

And that was one week and one day after I had just buried my mother. Not a good month.

Now there was a great opportunity for self-pity. If I worked it real good and manipulated everybody real well, I could have all of them crying, and we could *all* be feeling sorry for Mike. Those are some pretty legitimate reasons to feel sorry for yourself. I wouldn't even have to work very hard to get those moving.

Let's go a little deeper. I've been working these steps for many years. I've been born again for most of those. There's an attitude that says, "Oh, I've been born again and everything's going to be wonderful! Life is just wonderful with no more problems! And we're going to just skim across the waves of life and be happy all the time."

Maybe that happens to some folks, but my little boat in the sea of life gets rocked now and then. The boat hasn't sunk yet, completely. It might get a hole here and there. But God keeps me floating, calms the sea, guides my ship … if I let Him.

When these things go on, I thank God. Because of my relationship with Jesus Christ, I do have God, His guidance through this program, and this kind of insight. He gives me wisdom into myself and into Him, to say, "Praise God—they fired me. It'll be a great opportunity for God to do something." I said, "God, I've got a wife and three kids. They've got to eat. You've got some problems. I don't know how You're going to solve them, either. But I'll suit up and show up—everyday."

Step One is critical

Step One is critical. It is the only step that you have to take perfectly. You do have to take it, and you have to take it perfectly. You have to admit that you are totally powerless and your life is unmanageable. Until you come to that conclusion, you're not ready or able to go on with the other steps and get anything out of them. So, don't go to Step Two and Three until you take Step One.

———— **STEP ONE - ACTION** ————

Now that you've read the Step One lecture, meditate on the words of the step for a moment. Read it to yourself several times.

**We admitted we were powerless over our human condition—
that our lives had become unmanageable.**

The simple purpose of this step is clearly stated in the step itself. This is your first step toward making peace with God. You do this by admitting your powerlessness over your human condition. This is all you need to do in this first step.

As always, begin to trust God by asking Him to bring to mind the honest answers to these questions.

A. *Taking Action*

Refer to the Addictions list and the Reality Checks on pages 7-9 of this book. Now answer the following questions:

1. Name specific things over which you are powerless as they come to your mind. Consider your emotions, thoughts, and behaviors.

2. Name the things that are unmanageable in your life.

3. List the things over which you have:
(a) power

(b) control

(c) authority

Note: During the time that you are spending on the first step, review these first three questions on a daily basis. Be willing to add to or change your answers as you make new discoveries.

4. What are the patterns of behavior that you are repeating that are causing your life to be unmanageable?

5. How have you tried to manage these areas of your life?

6. Describe some of your obsessive thinking; that is, how your mind repeatedly thinks about these addictions or patterns of behavior.

7. List how you rationalize your addictions and/or harmful patterns of behaviors.

8. What has caused the blocking of God's Spirit in your life?

9. What medicators do you use to feel good? (By medicators, I mean those things that cover over the bad feelings or the pain—those things that help make it go away.)

10. In what ways have you been dishonest with yourself?

11. List the consequences of your addictions, compulsive behavior, and self-defeating life patterns.

12. How has your behavior affected others?

13. How have your best efforts resulted in changing these areas of your life?

14. Are you ready to admit that without God you are powerless and your life is unmanageable?   If so, then you are ready to take the first step.

Sincerely pray: "Dear God, I, _____, admit I am powerless over my human condition—that my life has become unmanageable."

B. *In your journal:*
   1. Be aware this week of the things that you are powerless over. List them and write your thoughts, feelings, and discoveries about them.
   2. In what ways have you discovered God or sensed His presence in your life today?
   3. What victories have you had today?
   4. What defeats have you had today?

STEP TWO

Came to believe that a Power greater than ourselves could restore us to sanity.

In my opinion, this is the most interesting step of all twelve. It's also more skipped over and paid less attention to than the others. People who have practiced these principles have misunderstood or not bothered to understand Step Two more than any of the others. One of the reasons for that is this: when most people read it—"Came to believe that a power greater than ourselves could restore us to sanity"—they think, "Oh, I've always believed in God, what's the next step?"

Even some of you probably thought that as you read it. But there's much more to this step than it seems at first glance.

I'm going to use a little bit of scripture, and I'll be referring to the book *Alcoholics Anonymous*.[1] The original unedited manuscript was written by Bill Wilson, the fellow who correlated the Twelve Steps. He derived them from six principles that came out of the Oxford Movement which was a Christian evangelical movement designed to evangelize the world. He attended meetings of the Oxford Movement during his early deliverance from alcoholism, and after about two-and-a-half years he decided that he couldn't evangelize the world, but he might be able to help some other alcoholics stay sober. So he split off from that and expanded those six principles into the Twelve Steps.

---

[1] You might want to buy this book and read it. It has incredible wisdom in it. It's difficult to read, but it's a great book if you choose to spend some time with it. The first 165 pages of the book are the basic study and introduction to the steps and how it works and about the guy, Bill Wilson, who put the book together. The book contains the original Twelve Step text, and I think it's a rather spirited text myself. I believe that God's hand was upon this man. He had a spectacular Christian experience and the experience is what he attempted to bring into the program that he was laying out.

39

Came to believe

Back to Step Two: "Came to believe" would indicate that we're going to come somewhere and believe something. One of the best statements that I've ever heard about the second step came from a fellow named Jack Boland, and I'd like to give Jack that credit—he's been working this process for many years. He said that *the essence of the second step is that we come to believe what we believe.*

Believe what we believe

How about that? We come to *believe* what we believe. Really *believe* it.
There's a difference between believing it and knowing it. We say, "Oh, yes, I know there's a God. Oh, yeah, I believe there's a God out there. Oh, yeah, I believe God loves me. Oh, yeah, I know this. Oh, yes, I know that scripture. I've memorized that. Yes, I go to those classes. Yes, I attend church."
Those are things we say and do. But coming to believe what we believe and really believing it, is a different thing—it's a different movement inside of ourselves. And one of the ways, or one of the avenues for us to begin to believe what we believe is to *stop believing what we don't believe.*

Stop believing what we don't believe

I know that you are intelligent people. And I also know that you have some discernment about you, if not a lot of discernment, and that you don't believe everything you hear. You don't even believe everything that you hear from the pulpit. There are times when we have to spit out the bones.
So, to stop believing what you don't believe is an okay thing to do in the spiritual growth realm. There are things in you and in me that come out of religious bondage of the past—spiritual bondage, religious abuse, cultic stuff, religious systems, denominational beliefs—different things by which we have been scarred and damaged that are either not the truth, or that are partial truths, or that are lies mixed with the truth.
Now, in order to come to believe what you believe, and then *believe* what you believe, you've got to figure out what it is that you believe. And then start believing it. I mean *really* believe it. And the way to start that is to stop believing what you don't believe. Just quit it. Stop arguing about it, stop talking about it—just quit it.
You may say, "Well, here's what I *do* believe. I believe that God's sovereign." Okay. Let's start there. Let's believe that—everyday. Let's stand in it and believe it. If you believe some more stuff, then put that in there with it.

It's always interesting when I come into a room of people to lecture. If I ask the question, "What do you believe about God?" Man, thirty hands will leap into the air. And they'll say, "Well, I'll tell you what I don't believe. I don't believe that TV evangelist is for real..."

and "The church I grew up in—well, I don't believe what they say, I'll tell you that..."

and "I don't believe in them tongues and Holy roller meetings..."

and "Momma always said that God was gonna get me and I don't believe that..."

and "I'm tired of all those preachers yelling at me—I don't believe a word they're saying..."

and "I'll tell you some more stuff I don't believe..."

They can do an hour and a half on your head about what they *don't* believe. But then I interrupt and say, "Excuse me. That wasn't the question. The question was, 'What *do* you believe about God?'"

"Oh, well. God, uh...God is love. Yeah, God is love."

Then I'll say, "Okay, thank you very much. Can you expand on that?"

"Ah...nah."

"Is that it?"

"Yeah."

But we can talk for another couple of hours on what they don't believe.

If you go to a bar (and I'm sure none of you have ever been to a bar or had a drink or anything like that), but if you go to a bar, the loudest table in the bar is discussing either sex or religion. And they're *not* discussing what they believe about religion; they're discussing what they *don't* believe.

So, habitually, we spend most of our time thinking about, processing, arguing with ourselves or someone else about what we don't believe. So, I propose to you to begin with this step: stop believing what you don't believe. Just stop it. Just quit. If you don't believe it, don't bother with it.

Now, at this point and for our purposes at this stage of the process, it's not necessary for you to have received Jesus Christ as your Lord and Savior. All you have to do is get honest with yourself and come to know what it is that you do believe about God and then practice believing it. You can't be where you're not, you can't be where you used to be, and you can't be where you're going to be. You have to come to believe what you believe and believe it, and God will meet you where you are, and, in that meeting, His power will change what you believe about Him.

And for those of you who are professed Christians and walking that out to the best of your ability, I submit to you, what you believe is going to change, too, as you move down through this process and continue in the sanctification that God has in store for you.

I do not believe the way I believed one year ago. It doesn't mean that I was an idiot a year ago or wrong or bad or needed to be shot. But as I continue in this process and continue to experience God in my life, I come to better understand Him as He changes me, and so my beliefs about Him change, too.

41

Power

Now, here's the principle behind standing in what you *do* believe, and releasing what you *don't* believe:

There's no power in something that you're supposed to believe, but don't.

Why? Because there's no relationship. For anything to work in my life, whatever it is, I have to enter into a relationship with it.

We can bring this principle all the way over into the physical. For example, if I'm an alcoholic and there's a bottle sitting on a shelf, I know that bottle has power over me if I drink from it. I can know that all day long, but until I enter the relationship with that alcohol—by drinking it—it doesn't have an effect on me.

It's true with people. Here's a person and I know that I care about this person. This person cares about me. Gosh, it would be wonderful if we could get together. That would be an uplifting, edifying experience; and maybe we could get married and have kids, and so on and so forth. And it's a great idea. Okay? But until I enter into the relationship with that person, there's no power in that relationship. That relationship just doesn't exist.

In the spiritual realm, God is exactly the same. The principles behind the steps are founded and grounded in a personal relationship with God as you come more and more to understand Him and grow in Him. That's it. Religion, in its original essence, is based on a relationship with God and then built upon that.

Any religion that is not based on a relationship with Jesus Christ as Lord becomes something that you suffer from, not something that you're edified by.

And there's a bunch of you out there that have suffered from religious abuse. I know I have. There were lots of beliefs and lots of stuff that I had to sign up for that I didn't know whether I believed or not. But I did not have a basic relationship with Jesus Christ. Therefore, the religious system and the religious works system became something that I suffered from, not something that edified me.

So, there's no power in something you're supposed to believe, but don't. The power is in *God* and God will meet you at the place where you *believe*. Remember, God meets us where we are. Not where we're going to be. Or where we were. God loves us where we are, no matter where that is. And when you get where you are and bring that to God, then you have opened the door for an honest relationship with Him. And those of you who have prayed a sinner's prayer and that kind of thing know what I'm talking about. Sometimes, instantaneously, there's tremendous deliverance in a moment like that.

Well, that's not the only moment when that happens for us in our lives. There is an ongoing experience and process. Everyday we need to meet God where we are. You say, "Well, I don't want to tell God how I feel." Why not? If He doesn't care how you feel, who's going to care?

Sanity

"Came to believe that a power greater than ourselves could restore us to sanity." Let's talk about "sanity." If this step is going to restore us to sanity, that indicates that we're insane. So, for our purposes, we're going to define "insanity" as *doing the same thing over and over again expecting a different result.* And we're going back to some things we covered in the first step.

There are things that we are powerless over. These things bring us to the point of having to believe that God can do for us what we can't do for ourselves (or to the point of having to look at the Twelve Steps or having to go to church at all or having to get help outside of ourselves). We have the revelation that in and of ourselves we can't do this deal. We are powerless.

In the Bible, in the fifth, sixth, and seventh chapters of Matthew, is recorded a lengthy teaching that Jesus gave which is commonly called the Sermon on the Mount.

In this sermon, Jesus begins with the Beatitudes—declaring blessings upon different groups of people. The first beatitude is "Blessed are the poor in spirit for their's is the kingdom of heaven," and that's the first step. That's Step One. You've got to have a brokenness, or a broken spirit, in order to start. And that's where Jesus starts. Those are the first words out of His mouth.

To me, He's saying, "If you want this deal, everything I'm going to tell you for the next hour (or however long He was there) is going to be based on this statement: if you're broken, or potentially a broken person, you're going to be able to hear and move into the solution, because I'm going to give you the tools in this sermon for living, for walking this deal out on the planet earth, for being in the Kingdom of God while you're in your earth suit." That's the essence of what He was saying in the Sermon on the Mount.

(The Twelve Steps is the Sermon on the Mount boiled down into twelve principles that, if applied in your life, will give you the promises found in that sermon. If you want to study a scripture along with this book, instead of making it real complicated, just read and re-read the Sermon on the Mount.)

Now, back to insanity—"doing the same thing over and over again expecting a different result"—and not getting it. That's insanity. The powerless part of this is that we can't stop doing the same thing over and over again, whatever it is. We're powerless to quit it. That's what we talked about in Step One.

A Power greater than ourselves

In the Big Book (that's what they call the old *Alcoholics Anonymous* book),[2] there's a paragraph that says,

"Lack of power, that was our dilemma. We had to find a power by which we could live, and it had to be a *Power greater than ourselves*. Obviously. But where and how do we find this Power?"[3]

Notice, this is a book written for alcoholics to help them get sober, and in it he sums up all of our problems into one sentence. He doesn't say anything about whiskey or beer. He doesn't say one word about—"When they invented whiskey, that was our problem. Until then we were fine." No, he doesn't say that. He says, "Lack of power—that was our dilemma." It was our dilemma before we drank, while we drank, and after we drank—or before we did whatever we did. Lack of power is our dilemma.

So, we have to find a power by which we can live. All of us. Alcoholics and non-alcoholics alike. We have to have a power by which we can live—a power other than self.

For our purposes here, we'll be talking about **self**—the power of self and the deception of self. The fall of man in the garden was acceptance of the invitation to deify self—make something of self. That's the essence of our fallen, human condition.

We have to find this power, obviously, but where and how do we find this power? That's where the second step comes in.

We stop trying to believe what we don't believe, begin to believe what we do believe—and believe it, and believe it, and believe it until we come to *believe* it.

There's something that happens inside of us when we do this, when we practice this. Especially if you do it in prayer and meditation—on your knees—everyday. And believe what you believe. And *stand* on it.

You've heard, "Stand on those scriptures, stand on those scriptures, stand on those scriptures"—and you try to do it in faith. But you read the scripture and think, "Well, that's nice for Bob, but it ain't gonna happen for me." Nevertheless, you read it and read it and read it. And a lot of times you get deliverance, but how much quicker and how much more deliverance you'll get if you'll go to a scripture that you really do believe.

Find one about which you can say, "I actually believe this scripture here. In my heart of hearts, I really, really believe what the scripture says. And I'm reading it, and I'm *standing* on it. I mean this is happening. I

---

[2]They call it the Big Book because the guy who wrote it was an alcoholic and alcoholics are extremely grandiose people. They like everything huge—if it's huge then it's good. In other words, we're addicted to "more." That's our drug of choice—"more." So when he wrote the book, he thought, "How can we get everybody's attention?" And so he made it huge. Large dimensions. He thought if they put it on the shelf in the book store, this oversized, *big book* would draw people.

[3]*Alcoholics Anonymous,* 3rd ed. (New York City: Alcoholics Anonymous World Services, Inc., 1976), p. 45.

have a faith and trust in God about this. I don't believe anything else in the Bible, but I believe this line right here. This is the one I believe. Even if I can't grasp any of that other stuff."

And things happen. They happen almost immediately. And there are some of you who have done that, and you know that it's true.

We have trouble when we jump over into the things we're not sure of. "Well, they *said* that, so I know it's true, but I'm not sure it's true for me," or "I'll read it," or "I'll try it, but I don't know."

If we come to believe what we believe, then God will make it possible for us to begin to believe what we don't believe.

Now, when we take the position that God is God and that we're not God, a lot of things begin to happen in our lives. They happen when we let God be God and us be man—or God be the creator and us the creation—or God be the boss and us the employee. We get things in order. He's above us in authority.

We take that position in the first step and in the beginning of the second step. In other words, when you boil down the first step, it's saying, "I can't do this. I'm powerless. God, You've got to do this. Help." And that takes us off the throne and puts Him on it. When we take that position and move into the principles that we're talking about on the second step, we begin to have some things happen. They happen as we believe what we believe and take the step.

In the process of working the second step, we will find that some changes begin to occur in us. I personally like to call these the second step promises. They'll give us road signs of our progress in the second step. The book *Alcoholics Anonymous* describes them this way:

"As we felt new power flow in, as we enjoyed peace of mind, as we discovered we could face life successfully, as we became conscious of His presence, we began to lose our fear of today, tomorrow, or the hereafter. We were reborn."[4]

So, what we're really talking about at this point is having a rebirth experience in Step Two. Those of you who have had that born-again experience know that there is fruit from that. The fruit that we're talking about here is the feeling that new power is surging into our lives. A *new* power. Not the same old power—not solutions coming from the same old place.

"We enjoyed peace of mind." Gosh, wouldn't that be nice?

And "We discovered we could face life successfully." There's one for you. Just discovering that you could face life successfully doesn't mean that it will happen today. Discovering that you *can*...would be wonderful. It would stop some of that ruminating in your brain.

Such as, "Well, I'm a failure."

"Well, I did this."

---

[4]*Alcoholics Anonymous,* p. 63.

"Well, I'm out of the will of God."
"Well, maybe I'll do this."
"Should I work over there?"
"Maybe I oughta quit this job."
"Maybe I ought to start my own business."
"Well, maybe I oughta divorce her and marry her."
"Maybe I oughta get him and get rid of this one."
"Maybe I..."
Just on and on and on.
"If I had this, I'd be that."
All that stuff.
If we're doing that, we're not standing and believing what we believe. Believe what you believe. Have a feeling that you could face life successfully. Get up and walk it out.

Next, "We became conscious of His presence." That's different than, "Oh, I've always believed in God, and I know there's a God, and I know God loves me, and, yeah, I'm a Christian." Becoming conscious of His presence means, I'm *consciously*, not *subconsciously,* but *consciously* aware of the presence of God in me and in my life. Practice that. Practice that this week. Just make your conscious mind be aware of God's presence in your life.

As an example, I never step over a penny. Ever. Because somebody said, "Every time you find a penny, stop and pick it up and acknowledge that that's God speaking His prosperity into your life." And I find pennies all the time now. I didn't used to—didn't even pay any attention to them. But now I do it all the time. "Whoa, a penny!" Do I like a quarter? Naa. Dollars? No. Pennies! I love the pennies. Why? There's more of them. I get to have that conscious experience of the presence of God in my life more often, because there's more pennies.

Next, "We began to lose our fear of today, tomorrow, or the hereafter," which is just about everything we're afraid of. Today, tomorrow, and the hereafter. And some of yesterday. Let's don't leave yesterday out. There's that old saying, "If I look back, they may be gaining on me."
Fear. Lose the fear. I'll bet you have some fear in there...bet there's some of you with fear. I've been doing this a long time, and I've still got fear—fear of other people, fear of situations, fear of facing somebody, fear of conflict.
We hate conflict. We want everybody to like us, and we don't want to get in an argument or rock the boat. We think, "If I say this to this person about how I feel, they may tell me I don't deserve to feel that way, and they'll be mad at me because I feel that way. So, I'll just pretend like I don't want to knock 'em out, which is what I really want to do."

Then it says, "We were reborn." I liken the second step to the born-again experience—the Christian born-again experience. For our purposes, I want us to think about it that way.

A relationship

I want to note that the third step says, "made a decision to turn our will and our lives over to the care of God as we understood Him," and I'll expand on that in the next chapter. But I want to mention it now because there's a lot of confusion at times about the second and the third step. Why do we have to mess with the second step? Why can't we just leap into the third step? We'll think, "If I'm powerless, I'm powerless. Yes, I know there's a God. Let's just cut to the chase here—move on with it." That's our tendency.

We're a doing kind of people. Human "doings" instead of human "beings." We want to get on with the solution—fast. "Okay! Turn it over to God! Great! God, you got it! You can call me—let me know how it comes out—you got the deal! I'm turning it over!"

God's not interested in that.

God's got a job, and you've got a job. You can't do His job. He *won't* do your job. *Your job is to desire and want to enter into a relationship with Him on a personal level*—because God is a person. He is a person just like you and I. Greater than you and I, and infinite—infinitely more wise and powerful, but a person, just the same. (That would bear meditating on.)

Let's say, for example, that I have this little group and let's say I'm God. And they're my guys and I'm God, and they come and holler out, "Oh, we're powerless, God. We're all powerless."

I say, "I know that."

"We want to turn it all over to you."

"Okay."

And then they say, "Okay, we'll see you around. We'll catch you on the back side."

"Oh, wait a minute. Where are you going?"

"Oh, we got life to live. We got stuff to do, people to see, places to go."

"Well, what about me?"

"What...well, we...well, I don't know...you can do whatever you want to."

"Well, you know what I want to do? I want to go with you. I want to be with you."

You see, I liken God to a fat kid with a football. Do you all remember the fat kid with the football? (Or maybe you girls had a goofy little girl that didn't roll her hair right or something, and she had all the dolls?)

God's like the fat kid with the football. He's got the field, He's got the rules, and He's got the football. And we're the guys on the block who run around and go, "Man, I'd sure like to play football, wouldn't you?"

"Oh, yeah man, but you know Rodney's the one that's got the ball and all the stuff down there, man. And I don't know. We got to go *be* with him, man, if we want to play. You want to do that?"

"Well, I don't know, man. I think I'd rather not—let's just stay out here and kick cans and cuss."

And we'll cuss him, too, and make fun of him.

47

Meanwhile the fat kid's running around over here—happy—and shouting, "Hey, I've got the football, I've got the field, I've got the deal. Come on down."

And we'll come—once in a while. When it gets bad enough, we'll step in and say, "All right, Rodney. We'll play with you."

"Oh, boy. Man, ain't it great, ain't it great. We're having a good time!"

Then we'll go, "Nah, I've enjoyed all of this, but I've had enough joy in my life. I need to be miserable. I have to go now."

And we leave and he stays back over there in his little field going, "Hey guys. Don't you want to play some more football? Where are you going, man?"

But we go off in our deal. "No, I'm *busy.*"

"I've got to *do* this."

"Have to *be* somebody."

"Have to *earn* something here."

That's just a little analogy for you. You can believe that or not.

(I need to say this: You can believe what I say or not believe it. I'm just another guy trying to walk this deal out like you are. These are some revelations that I've tripped over in my own walk with God, and I'm just sharing them with you. It's how I understand God. You can agree with me or not agree with me.)

"That" and "could"

The second step uses the word "that" and the word "could." It says, "Came to believe *that* a power greater than ourselves *could* restore us to sanity."

"That" indicates motion. *That* God is going to do something. *That* a power is going to do something. It doesn't say, "we believe *in* a power." It says that we believe *that* a power is going to do something. Not "*in* a power."

"Oh, I believe in God." No. "I believe *that* God and *that* power is going to *do* that thing." Yes. And practice believing that.

What does the word "could" indicate? It implies possibility. Maybe so, maybe not. It doesn't say "would." So, what does that indicate? It indicates *that* something might happen "if."

What else? It indicates **conditions**. What are those conditions? Those conditions are what I have to fulfill to allow God to do His job and His work in me. It's just like standing on opposite sides of the door, with Jesus knocking at the door of your heart—there's some things *you* have to do to allow God to enter into your heart. If you don't fulfill those conditions, you stay on one side of the door, and Jesus stays on the other.

The only thing we can do is choose, *if* we've been restored to being able to choose. My part is to pray for the restoration of my will power, so that I can stand at that door and choose Him, daily and moment to moment throughout the day, and let *Him* do for me what I have *never* been able to do for myself.

So, the conditions of this step are what we've already talked about:
Believe what you believe about God.
Stop arguing and ruminating about what you don't believe, because there's no power in what you're supposed to believe but don't.
And there's no relationship with God in an idea. God is *not* an idea. He is a person. He's the fat kid with the football. He wants to play ball. Get in the game with Him.

Believe what you believe and have the experience in the second step. The result of that will be those promises that we read: new power, freedom, peace of mind, facing life on life's terms.

——— **STEP TWO - ACTION** ———

In Step One you admitted you were powerless over your human condition—that your life had become unmanageable. In Step Two you come to discover and believe in that Power that is greater than yourself and begin to build trust in Him. How do you come to God? The only way you can come to God is the way that you are. So, stop believing what you don't believe and really believe what you do believe, then start believing what you really do believe everyday.

Meditate on the words of the step for a few moments before going on.

Came to believe that a Power greater than ourselves could restore us to sanity.

There are two things I want to see happen for you in this step. I want you to come to terms with the actual things you believe or don't believe about God. And more importantly, I want you to begin to sense that new relationship that should be occurring between you and God.

This is a new relationship. Whether you've had an awareness of God's presence in your life or whether you consider yourself born again or not, this is a new relationship that should be occurring in the process of taking these steps. This process should take you to a deeper level with God where you come to experience the concrete, actual, hands-on feelings of this relationship. You will become aware of the day-to-day, moment-by-moment relationship you have with God. I want to sensitize you to that.

It's impossible to come this far and not have some revelations. Finding out what you are powerless over in Step One is a major revelation in itself. In taking Step Two, you should be experiencing some things that not only make you aware of a power greater than yourself, but will bring you into a budding, new, and trusting relationship with this power.

The following questions, hopefully, will guide you into a better understanding of what you really believe and don't believe about God now, and what is happening that's new in your relationship with God.

A. *Taking Action*

Take your time in answering each question. You may find yourself coming back to them later on, adding or deleting things as you are able to understand your true feelings, thoughts, and experiences.

    1. What have you been asked to believe about God that you don't believe?

2. What *do* you believe about God?

3. What things has God already done in your life since you started taking these steps?

4. How have these things given you a new awareness of the presence of God in your life?

5. What things are going on inside you that cause you to come to a new understanding about God?

6. How have you changed what you believe about God as the result of a new awareness of the presence of God in your life?

7. What are the characteristics of the God that you are coming to understand?

8. Have these characteristics of God changed your relationship with Him? If so, how does that relate to your recovery?

9. How would you describe your present relationship with God? Are you coming to trust Him more? Are some fears beginning to fall away?

10. Describe how you feel about this new relationship that is occurring between you and God?

11. What kind of a relationship do you think God is wanting to have with you?

12. What kind of a relationship do you want to have with God?

13. Are you feeling a rebirth in your spirit coming from God? If so, describe that.

14. From what has God already restored you to sanity as you've gone through this process up to now?

15. What are you going to do with this new information from and about God?

16. Are you truly beginning to believe that God can restore you to His sanity?

If so, take the step. Sincerely declare:
I, _____, have come to believe that a power greater than myself can restore me to sanity.

B. *In your journal:*
1. What things have you noticed about this step as it relates to you in your personal life, your relationship with your mate, other members of your family, work arena, friendships, money matters, etc.?
2. In what ways have you discovered God or sensed His presence in your life? The more we experience God in our lives, the more we come to believe in Him and to trust in His power in our lives.
3. What victories have you had?
4. What defeats have you had?

Made a decision to turn our will and our lives over to the care of God as we understood Him.

People misunderstand this step about as much as they misunderstand Step Two.

Made a decision

We take this step after having made a decision. The step is based on a decision or a movement of the will. And that move and that decision happens in an instant.

In discussing this step, folks are always saying, "Well, I'm spending a lot of time working on the third step." Actually, they're not spending very much time on the third step, because all they have to do is either decide or not decide.

The time that they think they're spending on this step is really time they're still spending on the second step. If we haven't made the decision to turn our wills and our lives over to the care of God, then we are not really on this step. We're still trying to come to believe that God can do for us what we can't do for ourselves and that we're going to let Him.

Another aspect of taking this step, or making this decision, is that it's a daily matter. I take the step every morning. Yes, I make this decision, and it's final, and that's it, and I reaffirm it, and that's the end of it—and I take about five steps forward and I take it back. I get up and walk out the door and *don't* do God's will in my life. Most of you will be able to identify with that.

Or I'll get into something and find out that I'm in my own will or in self, and I have to stop and go back and say, "No, I thought I made that decision. I thought I willed God's will."

Sometimes it's hard to discern God's will. It's a daily dilemma: "Am I in God's will or am I not?" That's an ongoing question for those of us who are trying to achieve wholeness through our walk with God. I'll talk more about that in Step Eleven.

Faith and Trust

In Step Three we make this decision to turn our will and our lives over to the care of God, because in Step Two we've been developing *trust*—not faith, but trust.

There's a big difference between faith and trust.

Faith is a *gift*.[1]

Trust comes *from* the gift of faith.

Because of our humanness and our human condition, **trust comes from experience**—that is, we develop trust through the experiences we have as we walk out the gift of faith.

We do not get trust automatically when we get the gift of faith. Theoretically, and probably theologically, we should. And, if we were "good Christians," we would get that automatically and do that. But due to our human condition we don't automatically trust God or other people, or other Christians for that matter. I want to talk about what that means in my life and maybe in yours.

Suppose I have just met you today. I have just now come to know you, and you want to borrow a hundred dollars and my car. You say, "Well, I'm having financial problems and my car's broken down. I really need that money and I have to have a car. And, of course, I go to your church."

I'm going to say, "Well, that's...uh...you know...I really don't *have* a hundred dollars...and uh...I...no. *No.* Sorry. I understand your dilemma and I empathize with you and...God bless you, brother. Let me pray for you."

But after I get to know you over a year or so and we form a relationship and I come to know that you are a member of my church and that you're a good Christian man and that you are responsible—and you come to know me and my family and we develop this relationship—then the same situation occurs, and you come to me and you say, "Look, man, I've had some circumstances happen to me here and I've got car problems and I need to borrow a hundred dollars. I'm running short on cash, and I'll pay you back next Wednesday."

This time my answer's going to be different. And the reason it's going to be different is because I've developed a relationship and a trust-bond with you.

It's no different with God. God is a person. God is not an idea or a

---

[1]Ephesians 2:8

theory. God is a person. And for us to trust, really trust God with our lives—with our will and our lives—the trust that we have for Him is going to be built on our *experience* of Him doing for us what we can't do for ourselves. As our experience deepens, so does our trust.

When most of us come to this step, we read it and think, "Well, I've pretty much done that. And just in case I haven't done it—yeah, I'll throw in there again and do that."

But when we take this step, most of us hold something back.

"Here, God, you can have this, you can have that, you can sure have the ex-wife (or ex-husband). I'll turn them over to you. You can definitely have the financial problem and you can have my addiction. But now my greed, and what I do with this right here—I need to control this. I need to take care of this."

We don't think about it like that when we do it. We just unconsciously do that. We hold on to the things that we want to keep control of, because we don't trust God for the outcome. We have a predetermined outcome in our mind of how we want God to interact in our lives.

"If I turn this stuff over to You, God—well, I'm having this relationship with this girl, and I sure want to marry her. She doesn't too much want to marry me yet, but I want to marry her and I'm turning this whole relationship over to You, and here's how I want it to turn out. We're going to get married in the spring. And it's all Yours, God—the whole deal. I'm not going to do one thing—just going to walk out my life and just be at peace with all this. That's it."

And we get up off our knees and run to the telephone, "Sally, what are you doing? What do you mean? Where are you going to be? I'll be there, too! …What are you going to do the next day? And the next day? Well, wait a minute. Have you thought about getting married yet? What do you mean, you haven't thought about it? Well, I want to get married in the spring. In the fall? No, I don't want to wait that long."

We just manipulate. She doesn't want to do what we want to do. God doesn't put it in place the way we want it put in place. So we try to manipulate the situation. Then we come back to God and say, "God, here's my plan. Bless my plan."

We say, "God, You're not moving fast enough nor in the way that I'd like for you to. I've gone to sleep every night and left a blank piece of paper by the bed with a pencil, and you haven't filled it out *yet* with the plan for me, so it must mean that *I* am supposed to come up with a plan for this. You gave me a brain, so *I* need to plan. I need to put this down and you need to bless it."

I heard my pastor say one day, "God has a plan for your plan." Man, that's great stuff! He does—He has a plan for your plan.

We make this Step Three decision once and for all—and then we remake this decision everyday—and then sometimes throughout the day.

The Care of God

Now, this step says, "Made a decision to turn our will and our lives over to the *care* of *God*." That means that He's going to care for us.

The scripture says that He has counted the hairs of our head.[2] It also says He feeds the birds. Why do we worry? He cares about them, how much more does he care about us?[3] When money's short and when things are not going the way that we think they should, we tend to wonder if God's forgotten about us, if He's left us out. Is He just too busy to talk to us? Why isn't He doing something?

If God wants to get my personal attention, He's got one way of getting it that is sure-fire, absolute, and instant. And that's through my pocketbook. All He has to do is knock on that pocketbook. My money gets funny, and I'm on those knees.

"Where's the money?"

"What happened?"

"What's going on?"

"What did I do wrong?"

"What did I do right the last time I had some money?—let's do that again." I'll go back to the journal and see what I did. You know, think and grow rich—what are the things that I did on that last deal?

That's one of the prime ways that He gets my attention, personally.

Wants and Needs

In this step I like to bring up **wants** and **needs**—separating our wants from our needs. It's a good idea, when you're wanting to do something or thinking you're being led by God to do something, to discern whether it's a want or a need. God says He'll provide for our *needs*, and we can have our wants out of our surplus. He doesn't say that He's going to give us everything that we *want*.

I have found in my own recovery and walk with the Lord, that everything I want is not necessarily good for me. I've also found that God loves me so much and is so merciful that sometimes He'll give it to me...and then He'll sit back and wait for me to come crawling back, crying, "Get me out of this! Do something! I don't want this! How could you let this happen to me?"

Some of you have children, and if those children badger you long enough—you know how it goes, "I want this, Daddy, I want this."

"No, no, no."

And they badger you on it, and you finally say, "Okay! Okay. Here."

Sometimes you're smart enough to let sonny have his way so he'll learn that getting his way isn't always the best thing for him. And in a similar way, God does the same thing with us. We badger Him long

---

[2]Matthew 10:30

[3]Matthew 6:25-34

enough, and He says, "Sure. Okaay...here you go."

And then there we go.

As we understood Him

Now, let's talk a little bit about the phrase "as we understood Him." This doesn't mean that we get to make up God any way that we want Him to be. This phrase truly means: as you come to know God—as you come to know about how God *is*. Not how you think He is or how He should be or how you wish He were—but as you come more and more to understand Him as He is and how He works in your life.

Many secular Twelve Step programs are little more than self-help programs. But it was never intended to be a self-help program. It was a God-help, God-can-do-it-for-me-because-I-can't program. Anyway, as this concept has become popularized in the secular world, the term "as we understood Him" as been taken to mean "as I want to understand Him."

This concept says that any kind of thing I want to use for God, I can use for God. If I want God to be doorknobs or coffee cups or trees or chairs or whatever, then that's the way I understand God. That's what God is to me. And, of course, my response to that is, "When the going gets tough, what's that doorknob going to do for you?" "How much power does that doorknob have in it?"

The A.A. text says, "(a) That we were alcoholic and could not manage our own lives. (b) That no human power could have relieved our alcoholism. (c) That God [capital G, *G*od] could and would if He were sought."[4] "Without help it is too much for us. But there is One [and that's a capital O, *O*ne] who has all [*all*] power—that One is [capital G] God."[5] It does *not* say that there are six or seven or twenty powers that have some power, and you can pick any of them you want to and understand it any way you want to understand it.

Someone has said that this business of "as we understood Him" has probably been the biggest problem with bringing the Twelve Steps into the church. Churchgoers don't like it because they think that "God" in that context could be Buddha or Allah or some humanistic concept, and, of course, these gods cannot supply and the program fails.

There is no power in those other powers that people turn their lives over to. That's what happened to me. I can talk to you about it from personal experience.

My experience

I got in a Twelve Step support group. I sobered up. But I didn't want

---

[4]*Alcoholics Anonymous*, p. 60.
[5]*Alcoholics Anonymous*, p. 59.

to talk to anybody about spiritual matters at all, because I was totally fried on spiritual everything. I had been in cultism, LSD, other mind-altering drugs, and lots of spiritualism.

I'd been in the spiritual world, believe me, but it was the dark side. I didn't know that it was the dark side, and neither did any of those other people who were in it with me. We thought that it was God doing all that.

So, when I sobered up, I didn't want to hear about spiritual stuff: "Don't talk to me about spiritual, because I've been in that realm, and I got burned. Talk to me about practical things—how do I stop killing myself?"

And they gave me practical things to do: "Don't drink, come to these meetings, hang out with drunks that don't drink instead of drunks that do drink. *And you don't have to do this to yourself.*"

That was a revelation to me, I'm telling you. When some guy told me, "Do you know you don't have to do this? You don't have to drink."

"I don't? My whole life I've been trying to get it right. You mean I don't even have to try to get drunk?"

"No, you don't have to drink at all. Ever. Period."

And that freed me—he gave me permission to not do that to myself any more. So, I just walked that out.

I didn't have God in my life. I didn't pray. I didn't do any of that stuff. I didn't take any of the steps except the first one. And that went on for about a year and a half.

Then I started asking a little more about God. "What's this higher power thing?"

And some guys started opening up to me. But the Christian aspect—"Nooo, no, no. I'm not having that. Not doing that."

But I found a group that looked real good to me—it was a cult, and it was big in the city where I lived. So, that was my deal. I ended up in that and in the whole metaphysical deception of it.

I was a "truth student." That's what they called it—a seeker of the truth. What made it so deceptive was that, I would estimate, 85% of what they told me was the truth. And 15% or so, maybe even less than that, was a lie. That's the trick. They mix the truth with lie, and they deceive you.

The spiritual principles that you walk out in that deception are laws of the universe. For example, the law of gravity—if you throw something up, it's coming down. And those kinds of universal, spiritual laws are the truths that they teach; and, if you walk those truths out, things happen to you. I mean they just do. The scripture says that the rain falls on the wicked and it falls on the just.[6] That spiritual principle is in place—God doesn't put the brakes on when an unrighteous person walks in a spiritual principle—it's still a spiritual principle.

So I was in that deception for about three years. And my experience fits perfectly with the deception of "as we understood Him"—the deception that I can understand God any way I want to.

---

[6]Matthew 5:45

Christianity

But remember that the original Twelve Step program came out of the Oxford Movement which itself was an absolute, Christian-based, Christian-principled program.

The statement, "God as we understood Him," was added to the Twelve Step program later. It originally said, "God," period. Simply, "Turn your will over to *God*." And others in the program said, "Well, we've got to soften that to make it more accessible." So it was changed to "God as we understood Him."[7]

Once again, it's God, period. One God, as you come to grow in your knowledge of *that* God. It's not how you want to make Him up, but that concept has been one of the things that's taken these principles into humanism and made the church leery of it.

The other thing that's made the church so leery of Twelve Step programs is the deification of the Steps. In other words, many churches, or Christians, are under the impression that people who are involved in the secular realm make the steps into their god. They are a substitute. Or their Twelve Step group is God. That's what they worship, that's what has power over their lives. And in some cases the church is right—that does happen.

Let's move on over into the Christian side of things and just assume that we're all talking about the same God and Jesus, and we're all born-again believers. We *still* want to understand God on *our* terms. We still have a tendency to read the scripture or read an insightful spiritual book or walk through our life and go, "Well, I think *I* know what that means—I think I know what God meant by that. And this is the way that *I* think that God wants us to understand Him."

The freedom of this step for us as believers who are trying to walk our spiritual walk in the Lord is to learn about what *He* says about Himself. Not what *we* say about Him. How does *He* say He is and how does *He* say He works in our lives. And we learn those things by reading the Bible and meditating in what God has to say about who He is.

To summarize so far:
>We take the step as a movement of the will;
>we reaffirm that movement on a daily basis;
>we don't do it perfectly all the time, but that's okay;
>and in that walk, we look for what God says He is like, how He says He works with us, and how He says His relationship with us is to go;
>and during that time, after we turn our will and our lives over, we get the gift of faith;
>and during our walk, we develop trust.

---

[7]*Alcoholics Anonymous*, p. 248.

Sermon on the Mount

I want to shift gears a little bit now. I want to talk to you again about the Sermon on the Mount, recorded in Matthew 5, because that is where Jesus laid out these principles.

First He gave the Beatitudes: He said, "Blessed are the poor in spirit, for their's is the kingdom of heaven." As I've already said, that's the first step—the powerlessness step. "I'm powerless in my human condition to do anything about myself, therefore I need God to do it."

Then Jesus goes on to say,

"Blessed are they that mourn, for they shall be comforted.

"Blessed are the meek for they shall inherit the earth.

"Blessed are they who hunger and thirst for righteousness, for they shall be filled.

"Blessed are the merciful, for they shall obtain mercy.

"Blessed are the pure in heart, for they shall see God.

"Blessed are the peacemakers, for they shall be called the children of God.

"Blessed are they who are persecuted for righteousness' sake, for their's is the kingdom of heaven."[8]

In the overview I talked about making peace with God, making peace with ourselves, making peace with others, and maintaining that peace. Then I talked about God's gift to the disciples—about "My peace I leave with you—that's what I give you."[9] Here in this sermon Jesus says, "Blessed are the peacemakers for they will be called the children of God." When I used to read that, I always thought that it meant, "world peace." I thought I needed to go out there and make world peace. But that's not what that means. He's talking about the same kind of peace both times.

This verse, "Blessed are the peacemakers...," means to be at peace with Him, at peace with ourselves, at peace with others, and walk and live in the peace of Jesus and maintain that.

I believe that the first beatitude, "Blessed are the poor in spirit," is a prerequisite for all those that follow it. In other words, if we recognize that we are poor in spirit (or powerless over our human condition), then we're ready to receive the kingdom of heaven (which is Jesus), and if we mourn or groan to the Father through the Son, then we will be comforted in our powerlessness. God will give us His Spirit to be meek, to thirst for righteousness, to be merciful, to be pure in heart, to be a peacemaker, and He'll give us the strength to be persecuted for righteousness sake. Then we will be at peace and be made whole in the Father.

Beginning in Matthew 5:17, Jesus talks about the fulfillment of the Law. He says, "Think not that I am come to destroy the law or the prophets. I am not come to destroy, but to fulfill them. For truly I say to you, until

---

[8]Matthew 5:3-10
[9]John 14:27

62

heaven and earth pass, not one jot or one tittle shall pass from the law until all is fulfilled. Whoever therefore shall break one of these least commandments, and shall teach men so, he shall be called the least in the kingdom of heaven. But whoever shall do and teach them, the same shall be called great in the kingdom of heaven. For I say to you, that unless your righteousness shall exceed the righteousness of the scribes and Pharisees, you shall in no case enter into the kingdom of heaven."[10]

Where is the kingdom of heaven? It's within—right inside us.[11] And where is it going on? Out there—among us. It's going on at some level here, not just in heaven "up there"—and it's directly tied to how much we turn our wills and our lives over to the care of God and, therefore, how much He is actively working through you and me and the other fellow as we walk around *here*. If you're here and He's here, and He's Lord, this is it.

We're not to sit around and wait for the rapture and go, "Well, boy, ain't it too bad" or "I'm glad I'm safe in here" and build the gates up around here and then do nothing. There are things to do in the kingdom—right now.

As I go on, I want you to stay in the "now" consciousness rather than thinking of the kingdom as something up the road in the future.

Jesus says that those of us who can adhere to the Law *that He fulfilled* will be great in the kingdom. And He makes the statement that He didn't come to abolish the Law, *He came to fulfill it*. Why do you suppose that we needed Him to fulfill the Law? Why do you think we needed Him to have the Law fulfilled in us? Think about it in regard to the steps.

What it means to me is this: "I'm powerless." I'm powerless to adhere to the Law. I have to have Jesus and the Holy Spirit in my life and in my heart to fulfill the Law in my life.

Of course, in my human condition I still fall short. I still don't walk a perfect life out in every area. But because of Jesus and because of His fulfillment of the Law, I am able to do the things that He lays out in the Beatitudes. In Step Three, in turning my will and my life over to Him, He does for me that which I can't do for myself. And that Law becomes fulfilled in me—and I in Him—and therefore I am able to walk out a place in the kingdom.

In the last part of these verses about the fulfillment of the Law, Jesus says, "I say to you, unless your righteousness exceeds the righteousness of the scribes and Pharisees, you shall in no case enter into the kingdom of heaven."

What do we know about the Pharisees? They were these guys that tried to do everything perfect, and then they just pointed and looked at everybody and taught them: "You do this." "You do that." It's a "doing" mentality, a

[10]Matthew 5:17-20
[11]Luke 17:21

"works" mentality. And Jesus is saying that if we don't get past that, we're not anywhere near entering the kingdom of God.

And you won't get past that if you're thinking, "I can read this book and I can learn about all these steps. I'll read those Bible verses and then I'll know about those principles and I'll know about the Beatitudes and all that stuff. I'll be very well versed in all those nice things. Because, really, the reason I'm reading this book is because there are so many poor, unfortunate people out there and I want to learn about this so I can impart this information to them."

But the way that this works is for each individual to go through this Twelve Step process and have this personal experience with God through these principles. God transforms you, or takes you to a place that you've never been before, and as a result of *that experience with Him,* other people can benefit from what you have in Him, or from that relationship or that experience that you've had with Him.

It's more than knowledge. It's the combination of revelation and experience in Christ. There's a scripture that says, "My people are destroyed for lack of knowledge."[12] So, there's not a thing in the world wrong with knowledge, but *people don't hear your knowledge. People hear your walk.* Your kids don't do what you tell them, they do what you do.

And so, for me, Jesus is telling us how to do it—how to put it into practice. In this Sermon on the Mount He gives us hands-on, practical, digestible things to do or understand.

"Yes, I want to repent. How do I repent and *stay* in repentance?"

"Yeah, I want God's will in my life. But how do I do that?"

"Somebody tell me exactly what to do, and I'll do that."

"What does God really want from me?"

That's the way we are as humans. We love those little formulas—those one, two, three, four steps to getting more money, five steps to happiness, ten steps to losing thirty pounds—all those kinds of things.

As Jesus continues this Sermon, He talks about murder, divorce, taking oaths, adultery, an eye for an eye. He goes through these laws and takes them out of the letter of the law and puts them into the spirit of the law. He moves it from the outward doing of things to the inward being of the new creature man.

For instance, murder: He says that you've heard it's wrong to murder; don't murder. "Whoever shall kill shall be in danger of the judgment. But I say to you, that whoever is angry with his brother without a cause shall be in danger of the judgment, and whoever shall say to his brother, Raca [an Aramaic term of contempt], shall be in danger of the council; but whoever shall say, You fool, shall be in danger of hell fire."[13]

And He goes on and talks about anger and sinning against your brother, and then He talks about having resentments and your brother having something against you. If you bring your sacrifice to the altar, you

---

[12]Hosea 4:6
[13]Matthew 5:21-22

have to leave it on the altar and go to your brother and make amends and then come back.[14] Well, we're not there yet, but down in Step Eight it's going to say, "Became willing to make amends to all the people that we had harmed," and in Step Nine, "Made direct amends to all of them where possible."

So, just as in these steps, He's pulling out conditions that we have to fulfill to adhere to His fulfillment of the law in us—actions that we have to perform.

That one statement about having something against your brother, or your brother having something against you because of what you've done to him, tells me, "Don't bring your prayer, don't bring your sacrifice to the altar—I don't hear you. I don't hear you. Don't come up here, kneeling down and saying, 'Boy, you know, Joe Bob—man, I really got a resentment for this guy. God, you need to do something to him. I want you to knock his teeth out.'"

David's always talking in the Psalms about knocking their teeth out. We kind of like that—you know, "Knock ole Joe Bob's teeth out and then I'll be all right."

But God is saying, "No. I don't hear that. I don't hear your prayer. I don't hear anything you're asking—until you go to him and clear that up."

That's a direct principle out of the Bible that's specifically in these steps.

And then Jesus talks about fasting and giving to the needy and loving your enemies instead of hating them[15]—which is another aspect of being at peace with people.

And all of these things are impossible for me to do in and of myself. *All* totally impossible.

Back when I was a youngster, I would read this stuff and they would preach to me and I would try to take it in and I'd go, "Okay. Well, I've got to act right and do right and then, God will be okay with me." I tried to live that for the first thirty-five years of my life. But I could never do that. I'll *never* be able to do that. He's got to do it in me, through me, and for me. I can suit up and show up, but I can't do that.

My third step - for real

When I was still in that cult, I had a physical problem and I almost died. I was lying in the hospital. I was bankrupt. My father was dying of cancer. My mother was on the seventh floor of the same hospital in the psychiatric ward. I'm an only child—no brothers or sisters. On the way to the hospital a woman ran a stop sign in a pickup truck and totaled out my van. My right lung was collapsed and they were going to do exploratory surgery on me—they didn't know if I had cancer, tuberculosis, or some sort

---

[14]Matthew 5:23-24
[15]Matthew 5:44

of foreign lung thing they'd never heard of. And the lung that didn't collapse was in worse shape than the one that did collapse. They walked in and told me they didn't know if I would come off the operating table alive, and, if I did, that I might be a surgical cripple.

At that point (and I was seven years into sobriety), God had my undivided attention. I had nothing left and there was nobody else to go to. That's when I decided to take this step—to turn my will and life over to the care of God. And God said, "Well, O'Neil, for seven years I've seen your program, and now I'm going to show you Mine."

Are *you* ready?

In the last chapter, we talked bout the promises of the second step that tell us that we are ready to take the third step. Those were:
> feeling a new power flow in,
> enjoying peace of mind,
> discovering that we could face life successfully,
> becoming conscious of His presence,
> losing fear of today, tomorrow, and the hereafter,
> and feeling that we were reborn.

So, in Step Two, we were beginning to feel the movement of the Spirit inside of us in a new way. Now, in this step, we can turn our will and lives over to the care of God.

Pray

This step needs to be taken with another person, on your knees, out loud. Make the commitment and pray a prayer using the words, "to turn my will and my life over to the care of God."

——— STEP THREE - ACTION ———

You may already be surprised at some of the things happening to you as the result of taking Steps One and Two. You came to terms with your powerlessness in Step One. Then in Step Two, you came to believe what you really believe about God. Now you are ready to act on what you believe. Meditate on the words of this step before taking action.

Made a decision to turn our will and our lives over to the care of God as we understood Him.

How do we know we are ready to take this step? In the lecture, we talked about the promises of the second step. Experiencing these promises tell us that we are ready to take the third step. Those were:

feeling a new power flow in,
enjoying peace of mind,
discovering that we could face life successfully,
being conscious of His presence,
losing fear of today, tomorrow, and the hereafter.

So, in Step Two, we were beginning to feel the movement of the Spirit inside of us in a new way.

A. *Taking Action*

The first three questions are designed to help you determine if these promises have become a reality in your life. The last three questions are to determine what you are truly willing to turn over to God.

1. What are some things that have recently occurred in your life that have heightened your awareness of God's presence?

2. Describe any feelings of God's power flowing in your life. Do you feel you have been reborn?

3. How have you experienced some peace of mind? Is there a new found sense of peace that you can now face life?

4. Have you come closer to trusting God so that you can genuinely make this decision to turn everything you possibly can over to the power of God?

To say that you are willing to turn your will and your life over to the care of God is a general statement. Think about turning over to Him such things as your money, job, mate, children, relationships, angers, resentments, lust, greed, etc., then answer these next questions.

5. What, specifically, are you truly willing to turn over to the care of God?

6. What do you fear turning over to the care of God?

7. If you fear something, then pray for the willingness to be able to let go of it and turn it over to God.

Below is a prayer for you to pray at this time. This step needs to be taken with another person, on your knees, out loud, in all sincerity.

Pray:
"God, I come to You as I am and I pray that You make me as You would have me to be. Relieve me of my self-centered nature as I now turn my will and my life over to Your care. Help me to walk out this decision in my life on a daily basis. I pray that you renew my mind and my heart, heal my body, bring me to wholeness in the Spirit of Christ, and help me to walk out these principles in my life. In Jesus' name, Amen."

B. *In your journal:*
1. What things have you noticed about this step as it relates to you in your personal life, your relationship with your mate, other members of your family, work arena, friendships, money matters, etc.?
2. In what ways have you discovered God or sensed His presence in your life? The more we experience God in our lives, the more we come to believe in Him and to trust in His power in our lives.
3. What victories have you had?
4. What defeats have you had?

STEP FOUR

Made a searching and fearless moral inventory of ourselves.

In Steps One through Three we made peace with God. Now we begin the steps through which we make peace with ourselves.

Step Four is a scary step for most of us. It was always a scary step for me. For we take a look at ourselves in a way that we may never have looked at ourselves before. We look at ourselves as someone else would look at us.

A window into ourselves

The drawing below is a window into ourselves.[1] It will help us to see what we're like.

As you can see, there are four different windows:

The **open** window shows how others see us and how we see ourselves.

The **secret** window shows things that we see ourselves, but hide from others.

The **blind** window shows things that we cannot see about ourselves, but that others see.

And the **subconscious** window represents those things that are hidden to both us and others.

Known to ourselves

open we and others see	secret we see
blind others see	subconscious nobody sees

---

[1]adapted from the Johari window

We have an awareness of three of these windows. We know what is in the open one, and we know what is in the secret one. We suspect that others see things in us we cannot see ourselves, but we are, nevertheless, blinded to those things. But the subconscious window is blocked—no one sees into it.

Two of these windows constitute denial: the blind one and the subconscious one.

We have things about ourselves that others see and we don't—no matter who we are and where we are and what we do—and we're in denial about them. Even if someone told us what they were, we wouldn't accept it or believe it. That's the blind window.

And we have things in our subconscious window that we have either stuffed down so far, or covered up, or lied to ourselves about, or pretended that they don't exist—that we don't even know they're there. And nobody else knows either. So, there's denial about the things in the subconscious window.

In this fourth step we are going to break through our denial, we're going to look at ourselves the way that others see us, and we're going to unblock that subconscious window.

How are we going to do that? It's very challenging. It can be fearful. And sometimes it can be near impossible for us to take this step depending on our denial—how blocked we are and how bound up we are in our **guilt** and **shame**.

Shame corral

The drawing below is called a shame corral (like a horse corral). A corral is something that holds things in, and sometimes it keeps things out. In that corral we hold feelings—all kinds of feelings. Some of us have *all* of our emotions in there.

Shame Corral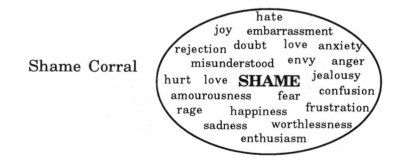

John Bradshaw says that our emotions are *"energy in motion."*[2]
E-nergy in **motion**

As we're growing up in a dysfunctional family, we are shamed about our emotions, or about our feelings. We're told not to feel, not to talk that way. We get beaten and start crying and they say, "I'll give you something to cry about if you don't stop crying." The kid is standing there hurting—he hurts and he wants to cry. It's the natural thing to cry when you feel hurt. And then you're told, "Shut up your crying or I'll beat you some more."
Those kinds of things.
If Dad's an alcoholic or a religious fanatic or extremely rigid—or if mother's a prescription pill addict or whatever—they have all these secrets in the family, and we don't talk about that. Dad passes out at the table, but we just say, "Excuse me, pass the potatoes." Or dad comes home in a rage and beats mom or me—and we just don't talk about that. We have the walking-on-eggshells syndrome in the home that says, "Don't make dad mad. He'll go off on us."
These kinds of situations tell that little kid inside there, "These feelings are bad," and it tells him that "I don't deserve to have these," and it tells him that "I need to be ashamed for having those feelings." This causes the child to be rejected. All rejection is abusive.
So, over a period of time, these things get stuffed into that corral, and a wall builds up around it. A "shame corral."
No matter what emotion or feeling that we have, since it's energy in motion, it has to go somewhere. So, we stuff it down in our corral. It shoots around inside there, bangs against the wall, and the emotion or feeling that comes out is shame. No matter what emotion we feel, it translates into shame because we've been told it's not okay to have feelings.
Now we don't like to feel ashamed. We don't like to feel bad or guilty. Remember in Step One we talked about, "I don't want to feel bad, I want to feel good"? We don't like to feel shame. So, we medicate the shame. We translate it into something else. Once again, it's energy in motion—it's going to go somewhere, it's got to process some kind of way and wind up someplace.
It might transfer into a sexual desire, or a desire to drink, or to medicate with food, or to get into a relationship, or to perform in order to be accepted—all of which can eventually surface as an addiction.

So, growing up we were told not to feel the things we were feeling, and so we locked them up in that shame corral. Every time that they tried to get out, we felt guilty and more ashamed, so we covered the guilt and shame by medicating with something and blocking them even more. This describes a basic syndrome that all addictions are wrapped around. But you don't have to be a drug addict to have this problem.

---

[2]John Bradshaw, *Healing the Shame That Binds You* (Deerfield Beach, FL: Health Communications, Inc., 1988), p. 52.

Here is a diagram of that syndrome.

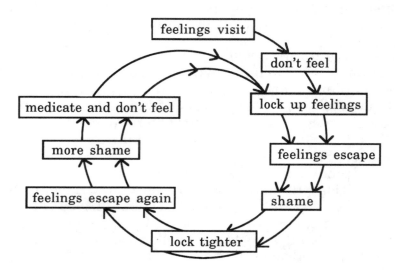

When I was drinking and using drugs, I loved Christians. Oh, boy, you could wear 'em out. You could just wear 'em out. Because we Christians don't know how to draw those boundaries. A lot of us, as Christians, don't resolve the guilt and shame that we're talking about right here. We don't get it completely resolved, and whenever a needy person comes up to us, we feel guilty if we don't give them something. What we may need to do, depending on the situation, is have the Spirit lead us in saying, "Well, brother, have you thought about the spiritual way of prosperity?...get a job?...has that dawned on you?"

Because of this syndrome that we're talking about here, we can't give ourselves permission to say "no." "No" is a big, ol' word. N, O. NNnnnno. Hard to come by for some of us.

There's a Christian guy that went through the Twelve Steps and when you ask him what happened to him and what good it did him, he jumps right up and answers, "I can say 'no.' I learned to say 'no' in this process." And I don't know if he even learned anything else. He just says, "I learned to say 'no.' And it's great." So now he's free to say "yes" when he really means it and let the Lord lead him.

A look inside

In Step Four we're going to begin to look inside this shame corral. And that's *real* scary. It's scary because everything that I have felt my whole life and that I haven't processed out is in there. Every feeling of resentment, hate, fear, anger, joy, lust, greed, embarrassment, hurt, loneliness, jealousy, rejection, worthlessness, confusion, sadness, frustration—all the way down the line—is in there.

Feelings are like visitors: they're supposed to show up, tell you something, and then they're supposed to leave. That's what feelings are *supposed* to do. But if they've shown up and we've said, "Oh, we can't talk about this. Come on in here, let me hide you in my secret, subconscious room," and buried it, then we've buried this feeling alive. These feelings don't die just because we hide them. So, they're in there, alive and well.

We feed them as we go along in life reacting to life's situations. We continue to re-feel these feelings in the shame corral which we aren't supposed to feel, so they translate into the master emotion, which is "shame."[3] The master emotion, "shame," binds the shame corral feelings. It's a never-ending cycle unless it's broken. The beginning of breaking this cycle occurs in the fourth step.

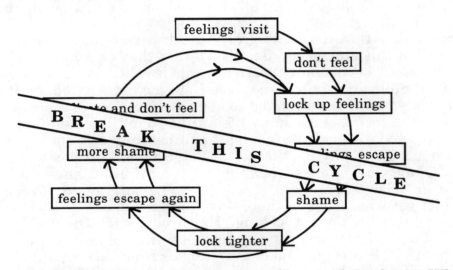

As we take Step Four, we're going to take a peek in there. When we open that closet, it's scary. It's *huge* in there. These things have been gathering momentum since the day they first came to visit.

Those feelings and emotions are like a bunch of caged animals growing in size. They've been in that corral so long that when we open the door, they rush for that opening. It's overwhelming to us a lot of times, and we can't take the whole thing on. So we jump back. We slam the door, and we jump back into our denial. We push things back into our secret, subconscious place, and we go on and pretend everything's okay. We might say, "Let's just go to church. I'll do something else, and I'll feel good about myself. Or I'll go do something for somebody else, and then I'll feel good about myself. Or maybe I'll just do a whole lot of things—anything but look in that door again."

Examine ourselves

This step works to get us inside this shame corral and expose the things that we've either been in denial about or that we've been keeping secret. We'll bring those into the light, and then, in Step Five, share those things with another human being.

---

[3]Bradshaw calls shame the "master emotion."

Lamentations 3:40 says, "Let us examine our ways and test them and let us return to the Lord." And 1 Corinthians 11:28 says, "A man ought to examine himself before he eats of the bread and drinks of the cup." So, self-examination is definitely scriptural.

However, there's an objection that seems to always come up in the Twelve Steps among Christians, and that is: "When I received Jesus, my past is gone away—it's taken care of—I'm forgiven, and I just need to go on. I can just forget about that." That's true. That's one hundred percent true. When you were born again, Jesus forgave you of all of this. He gave you permission to be released from all of it, and you can just go on and be a new creature in Christ.

The problem is that *you* won't give yourself permission to forgive yourself for all of this and go on. So, it's *not God* that's holding you back— or it's not that your born-again experience was invalid. It's totally valid. But because of guilt and shame—because I am a shame-based, guilty person and I have been programmed to believe that—I cannot accept that forgiveness in the secret areas of my life until I go in there and face those little devils and have Jesus grab 'em by the throat and jerk 'em out of there.

Now I don't know why it's that way. Believe me, I always wanted my deal to be, "Okay, God. Here's what I found out. You can have this. I'm turning it over. Here's who I am. I'm going to be born again. Come on in there and just get whatever's in there—don't tell me about it. Don't show it to me—just get it while I'm not looking. Have you got it? Okay! Here I am—I'm all fixed." Because I can't stand the feeling of having to face this stuff. It's painful. But there's no delivery for us from this stuff until we face it and forgive ourselves and give Jesus permission to rid us of it.

Until we do that we're holding on to layers upon layers of costumes or coverings, just as Adam and Eve covered themselves with the fig leaves. So as we peel off these coverings and costumes, we automatically become who we are in Christ Jesus without having to *do* anything.

As a new creature in Christ Jesus we are given the keys to the Kingdom and access to the power of God that worked in and through Jesus. In order to demonstrate the working of this power in eliminating our defects and peeling off the coverings we have accumulated, we must identify the defects, demons, or lies about ourselves and call them out one by one in the name of Jesus.

When we call them out, we must call them out by name. I don't know why it's that way, it just is.

When Jesus walked the earth there was a time when He found a guy so bound up with demons that he'd gash himself with rocks, and when they tried to hold him down with chains, he'd break them—so he ended up living in a cemetery. When Jesus saw him and started telling the demon to leave, the man got down and started begging Jesus to quit tormenting him. So, Jesus says to him (or to the demon, really), "What's your name?" And the fellow said, "Legion" (which is about 2,000 or more soldiers), because there were so many demons in him. It wasn't until the name of that demon was called out that they all left this guy.[4]

There was also a time when a blind man kept saying to Jesus, "Have mercy on me," and Jesus said, "What do you want?" Well, you know, this is *God*—He knows what's wrong with the guy. Everybody around knew the guy was blind. But Jesus wants to hear it from him—"What do you want?" Then the man admits his defect by saying, "I want to see," and Jesus says, in effect, "Your faith's got it, man."[5]

The problem we have is that we either want to deny that this defect exists, or we're too scared to look at it and to bring it to Him and ask Him to deliver us from it. After all, if we're a new creature in Christ, we're ashamed to be less than perfect. And some of us won't go to him because we don't feel we deserve to be delivered.

If you remember, back in the overview I told you that Steps Four, Five, Six, and Seven are where we make peace with ourselves. In Steps One, Two, and Three we've made peace with God. So we've got God, and as we move into the inventory, it's time for us to make peace with ourselves and forgive ourselves—because God cannot do what He wants to do through us while we're hanging on to all this baggage.

Write it down

Now, how am I going to do this? What's going to make it okay for me to crack the door on that shame corral when all of those horrible, nasty things of the past are going to come out and get me?

Here's the procedure:

You'll need a **pen** and **paper**. I recommend that you use a spiral notebook. Get the pen and get the paper, and get **alone** by yourself.

Next, number the paper, labeling the first section of pages from 0-6 years of age. Later, when you finish with this section, label the next section from 7-12, then the next one 13-18, and so on until you come to how old you are right now.

Then **pray.** "God, I'm powerless to take my inventory. But I believe that you could show me what I need to write, and I'm willing to write it down."

Then begin to **write**.

(It doesn't matter if you do this inventory all at one time or during many sessions. It will work every time that you sit down with that pencil and paper. Pray: "I'm powerless to take this inventory. God, show me what I need to know about myself. I'm on age eight." And just start writing.)

---

[4]Mark 5:1-29
[5]Mark 10:46-52

I want you to start at zero, or as far back as you can remember, and start writing. **Start with the first feeling** that you ever remember having— the feeling you had at age one, two, three, or whatever it was.

My first feeling that I remember in my whole life was fear. That's the first emotion that I ever felt. Not love, fear. Now I'm not saying that there wasn't love there or people weren't loving me or whatever they were doing—I'm just telling you that the first feeling that I remember having was fear. My daddy scared me; my momma and their fighting scared me. I was just a little bitty guy—maybe two years old. And my house was scary. So fear was the first emotion that I remember having. My parents were big and supposed to know everything—they were like God to me—I didn't know anything about God. And I was afraid to tell them that I was afraid. So, at two years of age, I began stuffing feelings in my box—putting feelings in that shame corral.

Maybe some of you did the same thing. I don't know, but look at it. What feeling did you feel?

As you write and begin to move forward, **look for your reactions to life**. Even though you were only zero to six years old, you had some reactions to life.

I had reactions. When mom and dad fought and I felt fear, I went back to my room and I closed my door and I hid. I used to go hide in my closet, get behind the clothes, and close the door. I'd get way back in the corner in the dark—and hide.

Write that kind of thing down.

As you move forward, look for **patterns of behavior**. Look for things that you did time and time again. These patterns develop in the years from zero to twelve. They are survival techniques we develop to stay out of the pain. As the patterns develop, they become more and more automatic. They become more subconscious, and we just do them—automatically. They begin to have a life of their own apart from who we really are or would like to be—second nature as opposed to first nature or natural.

We begin to develop a false self. This false self enters into relationships with others—generally with others who are also shame-bound and are relating to others from their false self.

So we develop a cycle. Something happens, I begin to have feelings, I'm not allowed to have feelings, I feel ashamed, I can't stand to feel ashamed—but I find out if I drink beer, or eat, or have sex, or fall in love, or go to church, or something else...I don't feel ashamed. And that all begins to happen automatically. Something happens, I feel bad, and without thinking, I just reach for a drink. I'm not conscious at all that I'm processing it through the shame feelings, but that's what I'm doing. I medicate or feed my feelings.

There's a child in you, and that child may have been told during this period from birth to age twelve that it wasn't okay to feel, it wasn't okay to talk, that love is conditional and that it's based on performance. If so, that child was abandoned and not nurtured. Those feelings were not mirrored. And abandonment, to a child, is abusive. So even though your father or mother may have never smacked you across the room, and they grinned and smiled and did phoney things with you all the time—they abandoned your emotions. You're an abused adult child, because abandonment is abuse.

Those kinds of dynamics leave us with that feeling of "I'm worthless"—with that feeling of "excuse me for breathing air." We develop the attitude of "I'm sorry I may be breathing a little of your air, but unless I just go ahead and die, I can't help but breathe the air. But I'll just stand right here, and then if you want me to do anything, boy, I'll do it—I'll perform for you. I'll perform for you, because I just want you to accept me. *I* can't accept me, but if you tell me I'm okay, then I'll be okay." (Codependents walk out the door and stop the first person they see and say, "How am I feeling today? Could you tell me?")

So, look for the patterns. An example of a pattern in the area of relationships would be the person who continually gets involved with addicts; first with an alcoholic, then with a religious abuser, then another alcoholic, then a physical abuser. The pattern is that this person keeps pulling people into his or her life who are destructive, and that sets the person up for abuse—he or she becomes a voluntary victim.

Another more subtle pattern is how you react to criticism. Whenever I used to get criticized, especially if the boss criticized me, I just quit—walked out.

Another pattern would be in the area of finances. I get a job, I get some money, I get drunk, I lose a job, I lose my money. And that repeats itself.

Those patterns are established in the first twelve years of our lives—not the drunkenness or addiction itself, but the basic patterns that lead to those things. Most of you will find that the only thing that's going to change from age twelve to later in life are the events. It's as if you can take the stencil and just move it through life—you just walk it out automatically in different years. The events may be different at age forty than at age six, but the reactions are the same.

Now, we're going to look for the reactions, look for those patterns, write those things out, and end up with whatever your present age is.

While you're writing, don't try to figure anything out. Don't try to examine yourself and don't try armchair psychology. The procedure of writing it down in the flow like that just generates the memories. You can go back and get specific about the patterns later. Just write. "When I was five years old, I was so mad at my dad, I hated my dad. I just hated him." Don't censor it. You may think, "I hope nobody saw me write that. I'd better erase that." No, don't erase it. Leave it. Leave it—whatever it is.

Not everything you write down has to be a revelation. You may just start writing, "Well, when I was eight years old, I used to have a pretty good time. I played with dolls, and I did so and so, and then I met Johnny down the street, and Johnny was mean and he stole my dolls, and I went down and smashed his truck, and..." Just let it roll, until you're writing, "and Dad found out about that, and Dad beat me beyond recognition, and it wasn't fair, and I felt anger, resentment, abuse—felt like he didn't love me." And then just keep writing. But be honest with yourself. The key here is self-honesty. That's what will bring you to freedom.

I don't want you to write anything in this inventory that you're *supposed* to be, or you're *supposed* to feel. I want you to write what you *do* feel, and how you *really* are.

There's an old saying, *"We're as sick as our secrets."* Your family was as sick as it's secrets. You and your relationships with others are as sick as your secrets. That's just the way it is.

This procedure of writing things down and letting them flow generates the memories. It enables you to go back later and get specific about the reactions and hone it down into the patterns.

Some things to look at

When you get to the end of this exercise, to whatever age you are now, then mark off a page for each one of the following categories and look for the patterns of behavior that have been harmful to yourself or others:

God	Marriage	Career
Religion	Family	Finances
Sex	Relationships	(add your own categories)

Ask yourself some questions:

God: How did you find out about God? How did you get introduced to Him? Through whom did you first see God? What was He like to you then? What is God like to you now? How does God work in your life? How do you feel about God? Are you happy with God? Are you happy with what God has done and is doing in your life? Are you mad at God? If God were sitting in the same room with you right now, what would you have to say to Him about how you really feel about the last years of your life? Would you be able to tell Him? Do you think God cares about you? Do you feel like you have a relationship with God? If so, what kind of a relationship? In that relationship, who does what? Do you pray? Do you pray everyday? Do you just ask for things? How do you pray? Do you think God hears you? What patterns do you see yourself repeating in your relationship with God?

Religion: How has religion affected you in your life? What difference do you see, if any, between religion and having a relationship with God? Do you have a relationship with God? How does religion fit in to that, if at all? What kind of baggage are you carrying as a result of religious abuse, religious opinions, or religious information that you were printed with throughout your life? How does religion affect you now? What kind of religious obstacles cause barriers in your relationship with God? Is there a place for religion in your life? If so, what is that place? What are your patterns of behavior that are the result of your religious imprints?

Sex: When did you first discover sex? How did you discover sex? What were your feelings when you discovered sex? Were they shameful? Were they secretive? Were you made to feel guilty? If so, how were you made to feel guilty? What was your first sexual experience like? How did you feel about it? Did you feel guilt? remorse? shame? Did you feel good about it? Did anybody ever talk to you about sex before you had it? How do you feel about sex now? Is there a lack of intimacy related to sex? Do you feel like you have any problems in the area of sex? If so, what are they? What are your fears about sex? What guilt feelings do you have about sex? Is sex fulfilling, or is it a duty that you perform? What kind of sexual behaviors have become a pattern? (Look at sexual patterns through your life from your first discovery of sex.) How did these patterns unfold up to the present time?

Marriage: How do you feel about your marriage? How do you *really* feel about your marriage? Do you feel like you shouldn't have gotten into it in the first place? Do you feel like you'd like to get out of it? Do you feel great about your marriage? Do you feel like God is in your marriage? What does it mean to have God in your marriage? What things about your marriage would you like to see improved? What have you done in your marriage that has caused your marriage to be less than what it could be? What are the things that you would like to see changed about yourself and how you relate to your husband or wife and children? What do you think God would say about your marriage? Why do you think God would say that? What self-destructive patterns do you see in your marriage?

Family: What was your family *really* like? How did you feel about your family of origin? How do you feel about them now? How do you *really* feel about them? What is your current family like? Are you a good father or mother? Are you a good husband or wife? What kind of things do you feel are missing in your family? How has your self-destructive behavior caused problems in your family? How do the things that you're finding out about yourself in this fourth step relate to the problems in your family?

Relationships: What are the patterns in relationships throughout your life? What destructive behaviors can you find on your part? What kind of people do you attract into your life? What kind of people do you seek relationships with? Are they healthy personalities? Unhealthy personalities? Are any of these relationships Godly, and how do they build you up in your spiritual walk? How are any of these relationships unhealthy or destructive? In what ways do you relate to people that you think are unhealthy or destructive to both you and others?

Are you in and out of relationships often? Do you go from one love affair to another? Are you unable to have a relationship with the opposite sex without having sex? Do you mask your feelings in relationships? How can you improve on how you have relationships? Are you able to be honest with people that you are in relationships with? Can you share your real feelings or do you present a false self to them?

Career: How do you feel about work? Do you like your job? Do you hate your job? Are you a workaholic? Do you work sixty, seventy, eighty hours a week? Why do you work seventy, eighty hours a week? Are you a good employee? Would you hire yourself? If you worked for you, how would you feel about you? Do you put in your full hours a day, or do you cheat your employer out of time and money? Do you do things like steal stamps at work? Do you have a plan for your career? If so, what is it? If not, why not?

Finances: What happens to your money? Are you always broke? If so, why? Are you responsible or irresponsible with money? Do you hoard money? Do you tithe? If not, why not? Do you manage money well? Do you have a financial plan for handling money? Do you have goals with money? Do you see patterns in your life with money that have caused you to continually be less than able to meet your obligations? What are they?

One more question: Ask yourself, "What are the parts of me that I keep secret? What are the parts that *nobody* knows about?" Write them down.

Remember, we're talking about an inventory. The same kind of inventory that is taken by a department store. The items in the store are not good or bad, they're just items that (1) need to be disposed of so that new, more saleable stock can be put in their place, or (2) need to be enhanced or better displayed so they can be sold. We're merely taking stock of what's in our store.

Amends, resentments, and defects

As you write your inventory, you need to compile these three lists: amends, resentments, and defects.

Amends: a list of people we have harmed because of our self-centered ways.

Resentments: a list of people, institutions, principles, or other things we resent or hate because of what they did or what we perceived they did to us. (I've been angry with tire companies, insurance companies, and things like that.) These resentments may be justified or unjustified.

There's going to be a lot of people you resent. And the bad news is that those people are going to be on the amends list, too. Some of the people you owe amends to, you're also going to resent—and you will not want to make amends to them because you still resent them.

Defects: A list of character traits that continue to cause us harm and harm to others. We're not looking for things like drunkenness, over-eating, or workaholism; they are only the symptoms of the character defects, such as:

anger	perfectionism	judgmentalism
resentment	self-justification	smugness
hate	rationalization	stubbornness
lust	self-pity	selfishness
greed	self-centeredness	self-indulgence
sloth	fear	intolerance
jealousy	anxiety	unrealistic
envy	approval-seeking	unreasonableness
procrastination	impatience	domination
suspiciousness	gossip	disagreeableness
pessimism	laziness	complaining/whining
depression	discourteousness	complacency
unkindness	ungratefulness	indiscretion
dishonesty	inconsistency	insincerity
worrisomeness	self-righteousness	evasiveness
tenseness	arrogance	despondency
irresponsibility	phoniness	over-compliance
insecurity	living in the past	panic
lying	living in the future	control
pridefulness	impulsiveness	manipulation
oversensitivity	aimlessness	violence
indifference	rigidity	

Begin these lists and add to them as you go along and as they come up, but don't worry about it. You can review and complete the lists as best as you can after you finish the inventory.

Consequences and a gratitude list

When you've finished your inventory and the other lists, review the work that you've done and make two more lists. You'll have done the hard part. These lists will be easy.

Consequences

Make a list of the consequences that have come about because of your defects and harmful patterns of behavior.

Later on, in Step Six, we'll be preparing for God to remove these defects of character. As we take note of the consequences we've experienced in our lives as a result of them, it will help us to decide that we're "entirely" ready to get rid of them.

So, think about how your defects and harmful behavior have caused certain things to happen or have caused people to react to you in certain ways. Here's a list as an example:

loss of self-worth	guilt	stress
loss of virginity	shame	lack of intimacy
loss of values	humiliation	sexual issues
loss of boundaries	rejection	abuse
loss of trust	isolation	physical problems
loss of self-control	loneliness	inability to work
loss of credit	blocked emotions	financial problems
loss of property	self-hatred	divorce
loss of respect		job problems
loss of spiritual connection with God		

Gratitude

As you wrote your inventory, you probably noticed that there were people in your life that were helpful to you or that inspired you to do a better job or be a better person. Maybe your sixth grade teacher was on your side when the bullies wanted to knock you around. Or you may remember a Sunday School teacher who showed a lot of love for you and made you want to keep on going when the rest of your world seemed like it was falling apart. Some of you have a boss that gave you a chance when no one else would. There may have been someone around who didn't do anything specific but was always an encouragement to you.

This is a good time to make a list of those people and begin to thank them. Don't forget family members—a big brother or sister, an aunt, or maybe grandma. Anyone for whom you feel a special "thank you."

Call them on the phone, write them a letter, or speak to them personally. If there are those who can't be found or are no longer living, say a special prayer to God thanking Him specifically for each one and the things about them for which you are grateful.

Don't let this last activity hinder you from moving on in this process. You can say your "thank yous" as you go along. As soon as you get everything written and all of your lists made, you'll be ready to take the fifth step.

A caution

Before you start on the fifth step, I want to say this: If you have been working on your fourth step—whether you have written little or a lot—you are probably finding out that you're not as virtuous as you might have once thought. As you move toward Step Five, the thoughts of sharing those things with another human being may be rather frightening.

So as you continue to work on Step Four, please don't think about the fact that you will share it with someone. Just write it as though you're not going to share it with anyone ever. Treat it as though you are writing the deepest, darkest secrets about yourself that you have—secrets that you've never told or written down or said out loud.

If, instead, you concentrate on the fifth step when you're writing the fourth step, you will have a tendency to censor what you write because the sharing of the fourth step is a very frightening thing to most of us. We think, "Well, I know about this, but I'll just leave this out. I don't think I want to tell anybody this." But it's important to write it *all* down.

——— STEP FOUR - ACTION ———

In taking Steps One through Three, you hopefully have begun to make peace with God. Now, with Step Four, you will begin to make peace with yourself. In order to make peace with yourself, according to the principles of the Twelve Steps, you are challenged to take inventory of yourself. Before beginning to work this step, take a few moments to reflect on each word of this step:

Made a searching and fearless moral inventory of ourselves.

All you are to do in this step is to make an inventory. It is not time yet to do anything with it. Just be open and honest and let your real thoughts, feelings, and behaviors be known on paper. Write as though no one else will ever read this.

Note: If you are in a small group, it is not necessary to share your writing or your answers to the fourth step questions with the group. You may, however, choose to talk about the revelations that are occurring in you as you write your fourth step inventory.

Before getting started, pray. Ask the Holy Spirit to bring to your mind all the things you need to write about, including those you resent, those to whom you owe amends, and your character defects.

A. *Taking Action*

In a separate notebook, begin to write your inventory according to the outline below. If you need to refresh your memory of these instructions, review them in the Step Four lecture.

  1. Inventory
  Ages 0-6 (write about your feelings, reactions, patterns)

  Ages 7-12 (write about your feelings, reactions, patterns)

  Ages 13-18 (write about your feelings, reactions, patterns)

  Ages 19-24 (write about your feelings, reactions, patterns)

  Ages ...   continue the six year increments until you come to your age. Add additional pages as needed.

Upon completing this portion of the inventory, you should have knowledge of all kinds of patterns. The next set of questions should help you to dissect those patterns so that you can more clearly articulate, feel, and own them. By the time you are ready to make your defect list, you should know the exact nature of your wrongs.

2. Now, mark off a page for each one of the following categories or use the spaces provided here and write down the self-destructive patterns of behavior that you've discovered.

Look at your feelings, reactions, and patterns associated with God, religion, sex, marriage, family, relationships, career, finances, and whatever other topics come to your mind.

Remember to be honest with yourself.

Ask yourself these questions:

a. God:
 (1) How did you find out about God?

 (2) How did you get introduced to Him?

 (3) Through whom did you first see God?

 (4) What was God like to you then?

 (5) What is God like to you now?

 (6) How does God work in your life?

 (7) How do you feel about God?

(8) Are you happy with what God has done and is doing in your life?

(9) Are you mad at God?

(10) If God were sitting in the same room with you right now, what would you have to say to Him about how you really feel about the last years of your life?

(11) Would you be able to tell Him?

(12) Do you think God cares about you?

(13) Do you feel like you have a relationship with God?   If so, what kind of a relationship?

(14) In that relationship, who does what?

(15) Do you pray?

(16) Do you pray everyday?

(17) Do you just ask for things?

(18) How do you pray?

(19) Do you think God hears you?

(20) What patterns do you see yourself repeating in your relationship with God?

b. Religion:
(1) How has religion affected you in your life?

(2) What difference do you see, if any, between religion and having a relationship with God?

(3) Do you have a relationship with God?

(4) How does religion fit in to that, if at all?

(5) What kind of baggage are you carrying as a result of religious abuse, religious opinions, or religious information that you were printed with throughout your life?

(6) How does religion affect you now?

(7) What kind of religious obstacles cause barriers in your relationship with God?

(8) Is there a place for religion in your life? If so, what is that place?

(9) What are your patterns of behavior that are the result of your religious imprints?

c. Sex:
(1) When did you first discover sex?

(2) How did you discover sex?

(3) What were your feelings when you discovered sex?

(4) Were they shameful? secretive?

(5) Were you made to feel guilty?   If so, how were you made to feel guilty?

(6) What was your first sexual experience like?

(7) Describe how you felt about it? Did you feel guilt? remorse? shame? Did you feel good about it?

(8) Did anybody ever talk to you about sex before you ever had it?

(9) How do you feel about sex now?

(10) Is there a lack of intimacy related to sex?

(11) Do you feel like you have any problems in the area of sex?   If so, what are they?

(12) Describe your fears about sex.

(13) Describe your guilt about sex.

(14) Is sex fulfilling, or is it a duty that you perform?

(15) What kind of sexual behaviors have become a pattern? Note sexual patterns through your life from your first discovery of sex.

(16) How did these patterns unfold up to the present time?

d. Marriage:
(1) How do you feel about your marriage?

(2) How do you *really* feel about your marriage?

(3) Do you feel like you shouldn't have gotten into it in the first place?

(4) Do you feel like you'd like to get out of it?

(5) Do you feel great about your marriage?

(6) Do you feel like God is in your marriage?

(7) What does it mean to have God in your marriage?

(8) What things about your marriage would you like to see improved?

(9) What have you done in your marriage that has caused your marriage to be less than what it could be?

(10) What are the things that you would like to see changed about yourself and how you relate to your mate and children?

(11) What do you think God would say about your marriage?

(12) Why do you think God would say that?

(13) What self-destructive patterns do you see in your marriage?

e. Family:
(1) What was your family *really* like?

(2) How did you feel about your family of origin?

(3) How do you feel about them now?

(4) How do you *really* feel about them?

(5) What is your current family like?

(6) Are you a good father or mother?

(7) Are you a good husband or wife?

(8) What kind of things do you feel are missing in your family?

(9) How has your self-destructive behavior caused problems in your family?

(10) How do the things that you're finding out about yourself in this fourth step relate to the problems in your family?

f. Relationships:
(1) Describe the patterns you see in relationships throughout your life.

(2) Describe how you engaged in destructive behaviors in your relationships.

(3) What kind of people do you attract into your life?

(4) Describe what kind of people you seek relationships with. Are they healthy personalities? Unhealthy personalities?

(5) Describe how any of these relationships are Godly and edify you in your spiritual walk.

(6) Describe how any of these are unhealthy or destructive relationships.

(7) In what ways do you relate to people that you think are unhealthy or destructive to both you and others?

(8) Are you in and out of relationships often?

(9) Do you go from one love affair to another?

(10) Are you unable to have a relationship with the opposite sex without having sex?

(11) Describe how you mask your feelings in relationships.

(12) What are some ways you can improve on how you have relationships?

(13) Are you able to be honest with people that you are in relationships with?

(14) Can you share your real feelings or do you present a false self to them?

g. Career:
(1) How do you feel about work?

(2) Do you like your job?

(3) Do you hate your job?

(4) Are you a workaholic?

(5) Do you work sixty, seventy, eighty hours a week?

(6) Why do you work seventy, eighty hours a week?

(7) Are you a good employee?

(8) Would you hire yourself?

(9) If you worked for you, how would you feel about you?

(10) Do you put in your full hours a day?

(11) Or do you cheat your employer out of time, money?

(12) Do you do things like steal stamps at work?

(13) Do you have a plan for your career?

(14) If so, what is it?

(15) If not, why not?

h. Finances:
(1) What happens to your money?

(2) Are you always broke?   If so, why?

(3) Are you responsible or irresponsible with money?

(4) In what ways are you irresponsible with money?

(5) Do you hoard money?

(6) Do you tithe?   If not, why not?

(7) Do you manage money well?

(8) Do you have a financial plan for handling money?

(9) Do you have goals with money?

(10) Do you see patterns in your life with money that have caused you to continually be less than able to meet your obligations?   What are they?

i. One more question
What are the things that you have kept secret that *nobody* knows about?

3. Amends, Resentments, and Defects:

As you write your inventory, you need to compile these three lists: amends, resentments, and defects.

Amends: a list of people we have harmed because of our self-centered ways.

Resentments: a list of people, institutions, principles, or other things we resent or hate because of what they did or what we perceived they did to us. (Include tire companies, insurance companies, and things like that.) These resentments may be justified or unjustified.

Defects: a list of character traits that continue to cause us harm and harm to others. We're not looking for things such as drunkenness, over-eating, or workaholism; they are only the symptoms of character defects, such as

anger	perfectionism	judgmentalism
resentment	self-justification	smugness
hate	rationalization	stubbornness
lust	self-pity	selfishness
greed	self-centeredness	self-indulgence
sloth	fear	intolerance
jealousy	anxiety	unrealistic
envy	approval-seeking	unreasonableness
procrastination	impatience	domination
suspiciousness	gossip	disagreeableness
pessimism	laziness	complaining/whining
depression	discourteousness	complacency
unkindness	ungratefulness	indiscretion
dishonesty	inconsistency	insincerity
worrisomeness	self-righteousness	evasiveness
tenseness	arrogance	despondency
irresponsibility	phoniness	over-compliance
insecurity	living in the past	panic
lying	living in the future	control
pridefulness	impulsiveness	manipulation
oversensitivity	aimlessness	violence
indifference	rigidity	

Begin these lists and add to them as you go along and as they come up, but don't worry about it. You can review and complete the lists as best as you can after you finish the inventory.

There's a form for making these lists on the next page.

AMENDS	RESENTMENTS	DEFECTS

4. Consequences and gratitude lists:

When you finish your inventory and your lists of amends, resentments, and defects, review the work that you have done and make two more lists:

Consequences: a list of consequences that have resulted from our defects of character and harmful behaviors. We'll review these as we take Step Six. Here's an example:

loss of self worth	guilt	stress
loss of virginity	shame	lack of intimacy
loss of values	humiliation	sexual issues
loss of boundaries	rejection	abuse
loss of trust	isolation	physical problems
loss of self-control	loneliness	inability to work
loss of credit	blocked emotions	financial problems
loss of property	self-hatred	divorce
loss of respect		job problems
loss of spiritual connection with God		

Gratitude: a list of people for whom we feel gratitude—those for whom we are thankful for making a positive difference in our lives. Begin now to thank those for whom you are grateful, and continue to do so as you move along in this process.

CONSEQUENCES	GRATITUDE

When you get everything written and your lists made, then you'll be ready to take the fifth step.

B. *In your journal:*

1. What things have you noticed about taking this step as it relates to all the aspects of your life?

2. In what ways have you discovered God or sensed His presence in your life?

3. What victories have you had?

4. What defeats have you had?

STEP FIVE

Admitted to God, to ourselves, and to another human being the exact nature of our wrongs.

Humility

Why can't we just take our sins and go to God like we've always done and say, "God, here's my sins and that's it. I don't need to tell anybody about this. I don't need to do anything. You just take care of it and it'll be all right." Or, "God, You know me and You know my heart and You know what I've done wrong—just automatically take care of it some way."

The problem with that is that it's not scriptural.

James 5:13-16 says: "Is any among you afflicted? Let him pray. Is any merry? Let him sing psalms. Is any sick among you? Let him call for the elders of the church; and let them pray over him, anointing him with oil in the name of the Lord; and the prayer of faith shall save the sick, and the Lord shall raise him up. If he has committed sins, they shall be forgiven him. *Confess your faults one to another and pray for one another, that you may be healed.* The effectual fervent prayer of a righteous man avails much."

This scripture tells us that we need to share these secrets, or these sins, with another human being. In doing so, we share them with God and with ourselves.

So, why do I have to admit these things to all three? Because deliverance requires **humility**. In order to get real deliverance, not just forgiveness, but *deliverance* from the things that have been driving our bus—from our addictions...from our compulsions...from our destructive behavior...from past harms...from resentments that we've carried—we have to have humility. And we won't get the humility required for deliverance unless we move through this process of admitting to God, ourselves, *and* another human being the exact nature of our wrongs.

Secrets

This process is called "revealing your secrets." Do you remember in Step Four that I made the statement that "we're as sick as our secrets"? It's true. We're as sick as our secrets. Every one of us.

Our secrets are one of the things that has us, as the body of Christ, bound up, unfree, and unable to move in the Spirit of God as God would have us move. And I don't mean the secrets of the historical church, I mean the secrets of the individuals in the church. We are in that bondage because of the secrets—either of our past, or the sins that we don't feel we can be forgiven for, or sins that we can't forgive ourselves for. It's because of the secrets.

In the overview, you'll remember that when we got to Steps Four and Five on the diagram, I said that this was the part of the Twelve Steps where we made peace with *ourselves*.

A lot of us who find that we need this process discover that we are not at peace with ourselves because *we* have not forgiven *ourselves*. God has forgiven us, but we haven't. We haven't forgiven ourselves—we can't let go of that baggage that we're carrying, and this blocks God's deliverance for us.

Admit to God and to ourselves

Now, after you've written your fourth step, there's a recommended procedure for taking the fifth step. It's very simple, yet it can be very difficult.

First, you admit it to God and to yourself. It's important to own that inventory. So, you take your fourth step inventory and sit down with an empty chair across from you, and, out loud, admit what you've written in that fourth step to God and to yourself.

That also kind of warms you up, or gets you on a roll, so that you can go to that other human being, face to face, and begin to admit what you've written in the fourth step.

This is a very humbling process. It's also a very cleansing process. This process is *not* designed to remove the defects. Let me repeat that. This fifth step is *not* designed to remove the defects. But it *is* designed to give you freedom from the burdens of the past that you're carrying.

I point that out because Step Six and Seven which follow are the steps that are designed to have God come in and remove these defects.

We can't do it

You see, what happens to most of us is that we have an experience with God. We ask forgiveness for our sins. We read how we're supposed to act or be as born-again Christians, and then we, in and of ourselves, go out the door and begin to try to act that way. In other words, *we* try to pull *ourselves* up, and *do* right for God. What we need to do is have God's new life do right *through* us as we first *be* who we are in Him.

"Okay, thank you, God, for your salvation, for coming into my heart. Thank you for empowering my life. Now what are the rules? What's the deal?"

"Oh, okay—here's the deal: We walk like this, look like this, talk like that, act like this..." down the line.

"Okay, I've got it. I've got it."

And then we're out the door—and we're a human doing. Remember the human doing guy? A "human doing" instead of a "human being"? So, we're out there doing, doing, doing.

The problem with it is that *we* are the ones doing it. Then a year later, five years later, whenever—we come falling into the pastor's office, in tears and emotional turmoil, wanting to kill ourselves, or having all these crazy thoughts and insane problems. Can't get victory over food, or relationships, or whatever.

"But I've been born again for five years. And I've been trying...I've been walking...I've been doing...I read the rules and I'm doing all that, but...inside...I'm dying in here."

And, in secret, once again, in secret, I'm thinking, or doing, all these other things. And I'm dragging all the guilt that goes with it.

The reason that is going on is because we have not allowed *God* to do for us what we can't do for ourselves. Remember, back in the first step? We are powerless. Period. We have no power, except to choose wherever we're going to get our power. We get our power from one of two sources: either God or Self. We have a free will, or will power. That will power is the power to choose where we're going to get our power. And that's straight across the board for all human beings. There's *no* exceptions.

Admit to another human being

There's several important things that need to happen in this part.

Choose someone

First, we need to carefully select the person with whom we're going to share our fourth step. Choose a person that you can be honest and open with.

Now this may be a person that you're never going to see again in your whole life. That may be one of the things that you want to think about— "Well, if I go to somebody that doesn't know me at all and they're never going to see me again, then I'll be able to do this."

But make sure that person is a person who knows what you're trying to do—someone who's familiar with the Twelve Step process or an understanding individual. I also recommend using someone of the same sex. You may want to use your sponsor if you have one.[1]

---

[1]For information about sponsors, see p. 6 and Appendix 1.

Women go to pastors and tell them stuff all the time, but sometimes pastors aren't the right guys to take the fifth step with. It's not "confession"—going to the priest and going to confession. It's a different process than that. It's different than going to your pastor for regular pastoral counseling.

And *don't* go down to the church on the corner and grab some little old lady and sit her down and shock her brains out. When you get to the third sentence, she's going, "You did *what?* Oh, my! I can't believe that! I didn't think *anybody* did things like that!" That's *not* the way to do it.

In my opinion, the best person to take this step with is someone who has already done this themselves. And preferably a Christian person who has done this themselves. They are hard to find, but they're not impossible to find, and there's getting to be more of them—for which I praise God.

Pray

Before you take the fifth step, you need to pray. Both you and the person you're taking the step with need to pray. Pray—out loud—both of you. "God, we're going to take this fifth step. Reveal to us what we need to know, and bring it on. Make me tell the truth. Release me from fear."

Don't hold back

Next, when you go into the fifth step, bringing your inventory, you need to hold back nothing. *Hold back nothing.*

In almost every fifth step that I've ever heard from a man (and I rarely hear female fifth steps because you need to do this with the same sex), a particular aspect has come up. They share all kinds of burdens and resentments, and then they come to a place where they say, "Well, I wasn't going to tell you this, but when I was in the seventh grade I fooled around with another boy." Now that's true of most of the men who have done fifth steps with me. And what I do is say, "Oh, yeah, I did that, too. What else you got? What's next? Have you got something really serious in there?"

The relief that comes from them admitting that is unbelievable. I have literally had people in the fifth step share murder with me, but want to hold back that aspect and keep themselves in bondage.

When we put that kind of emphasis on certain things in our lives, it keeps us in bondage and under Satan's rule. I'm just going to tell you, that's the way it is. If Satan can get you to keep a secret, he can run your show. Any time he wants to...*any time he wants to.* He'll let you walk and look like a Christian, you'll just be moving along—you may get your own TV evangelist show all over the world—and then he'll look at his watch and say, "Well, it's gettin' about time to pull his string." And with one sentence he'll run your show...because of your secrets.

That's one reason this step is so important. I don't recommend this because of the shock it would be, but we need to be so free in Christ Jesus after we have taken these Twelve Steps that we could walk up to the congregation in our church and read that fourth step to them, word for word. And say, "Praise God! If someone can't accept that, they've got a problem. I don't. God forgave me, I forgave me, I've shared this with another person, here's my secrets. Embrace me or reject me, but don't judge me!" That's the kind of freedom that Jesus Christ wants His body to be walking in daily.

Feedback

Now, as we go through the reading of the fourth step to the person that we have selected to hear it, we need to be getting some feedback. This person should be careful to keep us on the subject, keeping us from going on tirades or tangents about issues that come up. There's a real tendency to get defocused during this process, so sharing with someone who has done this before will help us stay on track.

(I have had this step take as long as eight hours for two days...and that was mine. I took it the first time, for real, after I'd been sober for eight years. I had taken some superficial fourth and fifth steps, but when I finally wrote the ninety-page one, and sat down with the guy and spilled my guts, it took two eight-hour days. But then some are sicker than others, and I was sicker than most.)

So, while we're sharing this fifth step with this person, they should be giving feedback and writing down our findings. And we should be writing down any additional insight into ourselves. You'll be adding to the three lists in your fourth step: resentments, amends, and defects.

I've never seen it fail. No matter how good a job we do on these lists in the fourth step, during the fifth step, it seems to increase. As we share, things come up: "Oh...I didn't know that I've resented Uncle Bob all these years. Now that I'm talking about it, I realize that I've really hated that guy. I forgot all about that." Put good ole Uncle Bob down there.

Then the amends: "Why I never really thought about how I harmed my mother. All I ever thought about was how she harmed me."

And then the defects. In the discussion during the process of the fifth step, somebody stumbled across...self-pity. "Why, I never had self-pity. I never feel sorry for myself. Why, not *me*."

There was a man who went through his whole fourth step and all of his defects and never listed self-pity, though his entire fourth step was centered around feeling sorry for himself. Everything he said to me was, "Well, they did this to me, and they did that to me, and...you know, I deserve to resent them and...poor ole me." He would move to the next deal, and the next deal. And then he said, "That's it. Here's my list. What do you think?"

I said, "What happened to self-pity? Let's go back and start all over, and just start with self-pity."

He said, "Self-pity? Well, I'm mad, but I don't ever feel sorry for myself. I can take it. I can cut it. Never gets too tough for *me*. Bring 'em on. I'm angry, but I don't feel sorry for myself."

Well, he wasn't doing anything, *but* feeling sorry for himself. The essence of his condition was self-pity. It was the emotion of choice. In other words, self-pity was the payoff.

One of the driving things behind why we do what we do—trip ourselves, or shoot ourselves in the foot, or continue in this obsession—is that we will eventually get our payoff which is to feel sorry for ourselves. And the only thing better than feeling sorry for ourselves is compounding it by getting you and John and Jerry and Joe and some others to get in there and feel sorry for us with us. And we're real good at that. We can package up a real justifiable story, get a hold of somebody, and say,

"Look, here's the conditions, here's what happened, here's the way it is, how would you feel?"

And then he'll say, "Oh, you poor thing!"

Well, I knew it! I knew it! We get the payoff—self-pity. Because self-pity justifies our actions. Or lack of actions. Or our reaction...to whatever it is.

When we get through with the fifth step, we should have the three completed lists: amends, resentments, and defects. The person that we're taking the fifth step with should review these and make sure that we haven't left out something or someone that we need to list.

When you get to the end of the sharing, you've got the three lists, you've finished the process...and you will instantly, at that point, begin to feel relief because you will have shared burdens that you've carried your whole life. There will be a form of deliverance at that point. There'll be a lighter feeling. Sometimes a feeling like nothing is in your brain—just kind of numb.

Promises

Here is what are called the Step Five promises from the Big Book:

"Once we have taken this step, withholding nothing, we are delighted." That's one promise. We're delighted. Wouldn't it be nice to be delighted? "We can look the world in the eye. We can be alone at perfect peace and ease. Our fears fall from us. We begin to feel the nearness of our Creator. We may have had certain spiritual beliefs, but now we begin to have a spiritual experience. The feeling that the drink problem [or our addiction problem or our compulsive problem] has disappeared will often come strongly. We feel that we are on the Broad Highway, walking hand in hand with the Spirit of the Universe."[2]

---

[2]*Alcoholics Anonymous*, p. 75.

Quiet time

When you finish the fifth step, you need to go, as soon as possible, somewhere with this book and read the first five steps and the scriptures that go with the first five steps which are at the end of this chapter—and then *be alone with God* for an hour, with no interruptions.

During that time God will most likely speak to your heart. The Holy Spirit will move on you in a very healing, comforting, and consoling way. This is a real important time in the process of the Twelve Steps. It's always been very special for me when I've done it, and for others as well.

During that time with God, review the first five steps. And if something comes up—if the Holy Spirit convicts you and says, "Well, you remember you didn't talk to the guy about that store that you knocked over in 1971."

"Oh, man, I forgot about that."

Write that down. And go talk about it to the person you took your fifth step with. Whatever you have left out, and it comes back to mind—something that you either inadvertently skipped over or you left out on purpose—you need to go back and get rid of it. Because none of these things—none of these secrets, none of these defects, none of these resentments—none of them leave automatically, ever, from anybody. They just don't.

We get them, we stuff them, we hide them. We try to pretend they're not there. We pray that while God's in there cleaning house, He'll get those too. But there's a principle that says we have to face and call out those demons or defects before they leave us.

I don't know why it's that way. I wish it weren't that way. I spent many years in recovery and in being a Christian wishing that I could just skip those things and not have to face each one of them. But I had to take Jesus in there with me and say, "Jesus, I found another one. Look here. Get him. Get him out."

I wish I could just go, "Well, Jesus, you know, I've been kinda stumbling a little bit, so, you know, this evening when I'm sleeping, just kinda come on in there with the mop and the cleanser and just kinda get those deals and when I wake up in the morning, they'll be gone. Thank you. Good night."

But I wake up in the morning and they're not gone.

So, we've spent our quiet time. We've reviewed our first five steps, we've determined whether we need to go back and add anything, and we're now ready. We can answer yes to: "I've built a good foundation here. I've done a thorough job to the best of my knowledge." We're now ready to move to Step Six, which is being entirely ready, or willing, to have God come in and remove our defects and our resentments.

Remember that I said to have *God* come in here and remove these defects. Not you. Not your psychiatrist. Not your momma. Not your wife or your husband. But *God.*

Warning

The last thing I want to discuss about the fifth step is a *pitfall*. We have a tendency when we finish the fifth step to say, "Oh, I know myself better now. Ah, I understand why I used to do these things. I have been freed from the burdens that I carried because I have said them out loud. I'm pretty much okay. And I understand what my behaviors were and why I acted that way. I have them all organized here in my little wheelbarrow. I resent Aunt Mabel, and here's why I do that, and I understand now."

Understanding yourself is only the beginning. You are just as powerless over these defects as you were over whatever got you to this process in the first place. Once again, you have to have God's power, and God's help, and *Jesus* has to come in there and remove those defects. If that doesn't happen, then here you go, or here I go again trying to do for myself what I've never been able to do for myself—to stop doing this stuff, to stop being this way.

This is not a program of change. This is not a self-help program. This is a *I can't, God can, I think I'll let Him* program of *exchange. Exchange.* I'm going to exchange these sins, these defects, and my human condition for God's condition, God's heart, and God's Spirit.

Steps One through Five

These are the steps and the scriptures that I recommend you look at during your quiet time with God.

Step One: We admitted we were powerless over our human condition—that our lives had become unmanageable.

"For I know that no good thing dwells in me (that is, in my flesh): for to will what is good is present in me; but I do not find how to perform good. For the good I will to do, I do not do: but the evil which I will not to do is what I do. Now if I do what I will not to do, it is no more I who am doing it, but sin that dwells in me. I find then a law, that, when I will to do good, evil is present with me. For I delight in the law of God which is in the inward man: but I see another law in my members (flesh), warring against the law of my mind, and bringing me into captivity to the law of sin which is in my members (flesh). O wretched man that I am! Who shall deliver me from the body of this death? I thank God through Jesus Christ our Lord." (Romans 7:18-24, paraphrased from KJV)

Step Two: Came to believe that a power greater than ourselves could restore us to sanity.

"[God] has delivered us from the power of darkness, and has translated us into the kingdom of his dear Son: in whom we have redemption through his blood, even the forgiveness of sins: who is the image of the invisible God, the firstborn of every creature: For by him were all things created, that are in heaven, and that are in earth, visible and invisible, whether they be thrones, or dominions, or principalities, or powers: all things were created by him, and for him: and He is before all things, and by Him all things consist. And he is the head of the body, the church: who is the beginning, the firstborn from the dead; that in all things he might have the preeminence. ...For in him dwells all the fullness of the Godhead bodily." (Colossians 1:13-18, 2:9)

Step Three: We made a decision to turn our will and our lives over to the care of God as we understood Him.

"I beseech you therefore, brethren, by the mercies of God, that you present your bodies a living sacrifice, holy, acceptable unto God, which is your reasonable service. And be not conformed to this world: but be transformed by the renewing of your mind, that you may prove what is that good, and acceptable, and perfect, will of God." (Romans 12:1-2)

Step Four: Made a searching and fearless moral inventory of ourselves.

"Let us search and try our ways, and turn again to the Lord." (Lamentations 3:40)

"Search me, O God, and know my heart: try me, and know my thoughts: and see if there be any wicked way in me, and lead me in the way everlasting." (Psalm 139:23-24)

Step Five: Admitted to God, to ourselves, and to another human being the exact nature of our wrongs.

"If we say that we have no sin, we deceive ourselves, and the truth is not in us. If we confess our sins, he is faithful and just to forgive us our sins, and to cleanse us from all unrighteousness." (1 John 1:8-9)

"Confess your faults one to another, and pray one for another, that you may be healed. The effectual fervent prayer of a righteous man avails much." (James 5:16)

———— STEP FIVE - ACTION ————

Having made a searching and fearless moral inventory of ourselves, we are ready to take the next step toward recovery. Meditate on this step before taking further action.

Admitted to God, to ourselves, and to another human being the exact nature of our wrongs.

One of the purposes for taking this step is to have the inventory mirrored back to you through another human being and to get the value of his/her feedback. That other person should give you additional, deeper insight into your own character and your own character defects. He/she should help you expand on your defects, resentments, and amends list, catching things you missed. He/she should pick up on behavior patterns and help you determine what you need to do with them, or what you need to let go of.

You should more honestly own your own stuff and even be able to dump part of your baggage at this time.

God is really in this process, and real healing takes place when one human being tells another human being his/her faults. It is scriptural to do so.

In Step Five we need to learn and experience enough humility (honesty) that the desire to return to our old behavior will be removed.

A. *Taking Action*
   1. The interview:
      a. Set a time and privately admit your Step Four inventory to God. You might want to set a chair opposite yourself and imagine God sitting in that chair. Talk directly to God about your inventory. Admitting your wrongs to God serves the double purpose of admitting it to yourself at the same time.
      b. Select another trusting individual of the same sex (your sponsor, perhaps) who hopefully has some knowledge of and experience with this process. Have him/her to read the thorough instructions set forth in the Step Five lecture.
      c. Set a date and get together.
      d. Begin with this basic prayer. "God, we're going to take this fifth step. Reveal to us what we need to know. Make me tell the truth. Release me from fear." Add to this whatever you feel is needful. It would be well for both of you to pray.
      e. Share your inventory, holding back nothing.
      f. As the other person listens, he/she is to make a list of resentments, amends, and defects; and he/she is to keep you on the subject.
      g. When you are through admitting your wrongs to the other

person, he/she is to read back the list of resentments, amends, and defects that he/she picked up on.

h. If things come up that you had not previously listed in your resentments, amends, and defects while taking Step Four, take the time to add them in.

2. Go immediately away for some quiet time.

a. Read and meditate on these first five steps and the accompanying scriptures.

Step One: We admitted we were powerless over our human condition—that our lives had become unmanageable.

"For I know that no good thing dwells in me (that is, in my flesh): for to will what is good is present in me; but I do not find how to perform good. For the good I will to do, I do not do: but the evil which I will not to do is what I do. Now if I do what I will not to do, it is no more I who am doing it, but sin that dwells in me. I find then a law, that, when I will to do good, evil is present with me. For I delight in the law of God which is in the inward man: but I see another law in my members (flesh), warring against the law of my mind, and bringing me into captivity to the law of sin which is in my members (flesh). O wretched man that I am! Who shall deliver me from the body of this death? I thank God through Jesus Christ our Lord." (Romans 7:18-24, paraphrased from KJV)

Step Two: Came to believe that a power greater than ourselves could restore us to sanity.

"[God] has delivered us from the power of darkness, and has translated us into the kingdom of his dear Son: in whom we have redemption through his blood, even the forgiveness of sins: who is the image of the invisible God, the firstborn of every creature: For by him were all things created, that are in heaven, and that are in earth, visible and invisible, whether they be thrones, or dominions, or principalities, or powers: all things were created by him, and for him: and He is before all things, and by Him all things consist. And he is the head of the body, the church: who is the beginning, the firstborn from the dead; that in all things he might have the preeminence. ...For in him dwells all the fullness of the Godhead bodily." (Colossians 1:13-18, 2:9)

Step Three: We made a decision to turn our will and our lives over to the care of God as we understood Him.

"I beseech you therefore, brethren, by the mercies of God, that you present your bodies a living sacrifice, holy, acceptable unto God, which is your reasonable service. And be not conformed to this world: but be transformed by the renewing of your mind, that you may prove what is that good, and acceptable, and perfect, will of God." (Romans 12:1-2)

Step Four: Made a searching and fearless moral inventory of ourselves.

"Let us search and try our ways, and turn again to the Lord." (Lamentations 3:40)

"Search me, O God, and know my heart: try me, and know my thoughts: and see if there be any wicked way in me, and lead me in the way everlasting." (Psalm 139:23-24)

Step Five: Admitted to God, to ourselves, and to another human being the exact nature of our wrongs.

"If we say that we have no sin, we deceive ourselves, and the truth is not in us. If we confess our sins, he is faithful and just to forgive us our sins, and to cleanse us from all unrighteousness." (1 John 1:8-9)

"Confess your faults one to another, and pray one for another, that you may be healed. The effectual fervent prayer of a righteous man avails much." (James 5:16)

b. During the hour of meditation, thank God from the bottom of your heart that you know Him better.

c. After your time of meditation, ask yourself some questions:
(1) Having completely admitted your inventory to another human being, how do you feel about it?

(2) How do you now feel about yourself?

(3) Do you feel you can now look the world in the eye?

(4) Do you feel like you can be alone and at perfect peace and ease?

(5) Do you feel like your fears are falling away from you?

(6) Are you now beginning to feel more intimacy with God?   How did you experience God in taking this step?

(7) Have you moved from having certain religious beliefs about God into now beginning to have a spiritual experience with Him?

(8) Do you feel like you have made peace with yourself and with God?

(9) Do you feel like the problems that have been plaguing you most of your life have disappeared and will not return?

(10) Do you feel like you and God can now walk hand in hand into the remainder of these steps and through the rest of your life?

(11) Did you take this step withholding nothing?   Did you tell everything that you needed to tell?   List the things that come to mind that you missed telling about.

If your answers to these questions are not positive to your satisfaction, you need to reexamine what you've written in the fourth step or what you have shared in your fifth step, making sure that you've been totally thorough and honest with yourself and with that other person. If you left something out, you need to go back and tell that person and release yourself from that. Nothing counts but thoroughness and honesty.

B. *In your journal:*
    1. What things have you noticed about taking this step as it relates to all the aspects of your life?
    2. In what ways have you discovered God or sensed His presence in your life?
    3. What victories have you had?
    4. What defeats have you had?

STEP SIX

Were entirely ready to have God remove all these defects of character.

In Steps One through Step Five, we've admitted that we've had a problem and were powerless over it, and we've come to believe that God could help us. We sought Him and turned our will and lives over to the care of God as we understood Him. We've written a moral inventory of ourselves, and we have shared that with another human being. And all of that is quite an order of activities.

It's been pretty heavy for some of you who have struggled with turning your will and life over to God, who have written your inventories and struggled with who you're going to take the fifth step with. It was especially hard when you actually got face to face with that person and told them all. If you've already done that, you know what I'm talking about.

When you bring this down into focus, into concrete activity, it becomes very, very concentrated and it stirs *all* of your insides, all of your being.

This process is designed to touch everything in your life and how you react to it. If you have something good in your life, it should improve it. If you have a good relationship with God, it will get better. If you have no relationship with God, you'll get one. If you're in a horrible relationship with another human being that needs to be broken, you may find freedom from it. If you're not in a relationship and you need to be in one, you may find yourself in one. If you have a job that you don't need to have, be prepared to move out of it. If you don't have a job, you'll probably end up with one.

So, we come up through Step Five with a pretty heavy order. It's a lot to ask anybody to do. It's a lot of activity and it's a life-changing situation.

Nevertheless, Step Six **"is the step that separates the men from the boys."** That's the very first thing that A.A.'s book *Twelve Steps and Twelve*

Traditions says about the step as it quotes a "well-loved clergyman."[1]

Let me emphasize that: he says that being "entirely ready to have God remove all these defects of character" is what *separates the men from the boys.*

The clergyman "goes on to explain that any person capable of enough willingness and honesty to try repeatedly Step Six on all his faults—*without any reservations whatever*—has indeed come a long way spiritually, and is therefore entitled to be called a man who is sincerely trying to grow in the image and likeness of his own Creator."[2]

One of the things that we tend to do as human beings is go for quick fixes. But Step Six and Step Seven are not quick fixes. We may have been delivered from either a desire to drink or overeat or some compulsive behavior in the first five steps. But now we're going into deeper problems— the habits that cause the obsessions, the patterns in our lives, the defects that we carry with us—and have God remove those.

We've been doing those things for a long time. Some of us have been doing them from the age of two, three, four, five, six, on up. We've formed these defects, or formed these patterns over a period of twenty, thirty, forty, fifty years. These are the things—the defects of character, the "nature of the wrongs" (or the root nature behind the wrongs)—that the fifth, sixth, and seventh steps talk about.

We and God, together, are going after these defects. This is no small order. We're going to battle some of these for life. We won't automatically be perfect—we may fall prey to these faults at times.

You can liken some of these things to sins if you want to, but if you do that in your mind, remember that the nature of the wrong that I'm talking about is *what's behind the sins.* The sin is the symptom. In other words, if you're doing something that's sinful, I'm not after the sin. I'm after the behavior, the pattern, the defect, the nature in you—the thing that keeps happening over and over and over again so that you commit the sin.

It's like Step Two

Step Six is like Step Two. Step Two was "Came to believe that a power greater than ourselves could restore us to sanity." This sanity restores us to making consistently sane decisions instead of insanely doing the same thing over and over again expecting a different result—but never getting it.

In both Step Two and Step Six you come to believe that God can and will do something, and you become **ready** for Him to do something about these natures of your wrongs and these patterns that have been driving your bus for your whole life.

---

[1]*Twelve Steps and Twelve Traditions* (New York: Alcoholics Anonymous World Services, Inc., 1981), p. 63.
[2]*Twelve Steps and Twelve Traditions,* p. 63.

Were entirely ready

Being ready is the preparatory step to Step Seven, which asks God to remove those defects. We would think, "Why don't we just skip Step Six? We've got our defects here; let's just run down and get on our knees and say, 'God, remove them.'"

Here's the reason: The key to all the steps and the key to your relationship with God is **willingness**. God is very courteous. He never imposes His will or His life on anybody. He has to be invited. And we can verbally or intellectually invite God into our life, but if our heart is not willing to let God into that area of our life, then He doesn't come.

So, willingness is the key that goes into the lock and turns it and opens the door. And *then* God can come in and begin to work and mold and shape.

Willingness

You've got all your baggage that you've figured out and you're moving it around in your wheelbarrow, and you can say, "Oh, now I know myself better, and now I know why I've been eating five cream pies everyday. The next time that I eat five cream pies in one day, I'll be able to really analyze exactly what happened, and *I* will attempt to keep it from happening again." But we are destined to repeat these patterns of behavior if we stop at Step Five.

One of the reasons that Step Six separates the men from the boys is because it takes a determination to move on and allow *God* to remove all these things. Most of us, if not all of us, are very willing to have certain things go away. We really are. But some things are hard to give up. If you're an alcoholic and you're lying in the gutter, you're usually pretty willing to stop drinking. But stop lying? Stop being greedy? Give up the lust? Give up worldly things? Give up habits that are ingrained for life? Let go of some resentments?

Resentments—there's a big one. "Well," you say, "my dad whupped me."

So? My dad was a jerk. He was an alcoholic, and he raised an alcoholic. I *deserved* to resent that guy. I *deserved* to be mad at that guy. And I used to think, "Now you're telling me to let go of that. I don't have to let go of that. Then you're telling me to be *willing* to let go of it. Well, I'm not willing to let go of it, either."

What do we do to get willing? We go to God, because He knows anyway, and we say, "God, I got this stuff here. Here's the list. I'm willing on this one. I'm *real* willing on this one. I'm *real* willing on that one. I'm kinda willing on this one. And I'm not ready or willing at all to let go of this one." Then we ask Him to help us to become willing and to do the thing in our lives and in our hearts and in our spirits that will bring us to a place of willingness.

Before these things can go away, we have to go through the exercise of being willing to let them go, because God will not come in there just because we're passing this way. In other words, we can't say, "I have ten things here, and here's seven of them, God, and I'm willing to let all seven of them go—but I'm not too willing on these other three—but while I'm passing through Step Six and Seven, get those anyway, will You?" It's not going to happen.

That's why, if you're not willing to be healed, if you're not willing to receive, no matter how many times you go down front and get prayed for on specific items, if you're not willing in your heart, it's not going anywhere. You have to be willing, because the door opens from the inside.

That's the only answer I have for unwillingness—to bring it to God and get honest. "This is how I feel, this is where I am, and I'm not willing to let go of this stuff—I need help to become willing."

I know a man who had resentment for his ex-wife that he was taking to his grave. He didn't care. He thought he was justified. It took a long time for him to become willing, and then it took a long time for it to be pulled out.

Enabling hinders willingness

An enabler is somebody who always takes care of things when the addict or alcoholic person gets into trouble, like the wife who smooths things over with the family and the boss when her alcoholic husband goes on a binge.

One of the reasons why enabling is so detrimental is because it helps people hang on to the things that they're not willing to let go of, and it interferes with what God may be doing to help get rid of those things. That is, the people who are being enabled in the addiction or in their problem aren't paying the consequences for their behavior or the activity that they're unwilling to let go of.

I partied and drank and did lots of things for a long time—whatever I wanted to do—but when I began living in a cardboard box down by the Missouri River and my rear end bumped on that cement a few times, I became a little more willing not to do that any more. I just needed someone to show me how not to do it.

But as long as I was playing music and making money, or the musicians were enabling me, or I was living with parents and they were enabling me and taking care of me because I could guilt-provoke them over all the bad things that my drunken dad had done to me while he was drunk—why would I want to quit? I hadn't paid any consequences for my behavior. They were paying them.

But when *I* began to pay them, I didn't last too long. I can tell you right now, I didn't live too long in that cardboard box. Longer than I wanted to, but I didn't spend years and years.

It's the same kind of thing regardless of what the defect or the behavior is that we need the victory over. We're very good at manipulating other people and getting them to feel sorry for us or getting them in sick with us on whatever our thing is that we're unwilling to let go of. We can rationalize and justify whatever it is that we're holding on to.

Religion versus Spirituality
(more baggage)

In Step Six, I like to talk about some additional baggage that most of us carry. I always bring it up because it affects our relationship with God.

When I lecture I ask the audience for definitions for the two words, "religion" and "spirituality." I write the two words up on a chalkboard and say something like this: "I want to ask you, any of you, to call out some definitions in your own words for these two things." This is the list that came up in a recent series of lectures. It's typical.

Religion	vs.	Spirituality
Form		Honesty
Ritual		Relationship
Control		Liberty
Rules/Laws		Acceptance
Works		Peace
Tradition		Forgiveness
Outward		Inward
Legalism		Compassion
Dogma/Doctrine		Grace

People always give the definitions for religion first, and they always tend to be negative. Then they give the definitions for spirituality, and they always tend to be positive.

It reminds me of what I told you in Step Two about people who want to tell you about all the things they *don't* believe about God, but are hard-pressed to talk about what they *do* believe about God.

What does this list tell you about how people feel about religion?

Any religion that is not first based on a personal relationship with God becomes something you suffer from, not something that you're edified by.

Now, originally, to be a Christian was to be in a pure relationship with God through faith in Jesus Christ. All doctrines and traditions are to grow out of that relationship. What religion should be is how one chooses to express his spirituality. Spirituality *is* the relationship with God. It has liberty, acceptance, grace, forgiveness, peace, compassion—it's an inward, personal relationship with God.

Religion has to do with how we express this relationship, nothing else. It should edify, glorify, and expand on our spirituality—not choke it to death.

The definitions on the religion/spirituality list were given to me by a room full of Christian people. I would have expected these definitions to come from a room full of alcoholics. They *always* start with religion first, and they bark out the answers. "Ritual!" "Control!" "Form!" "Rules!" "Government!" "Grrrr!" "Awrrr!"

But "spirituality is wonderful..."

I believe this exercise shows that something is going on inside of each and everyone of us in regard to religion, or how we approach God in our relationship with Him.

First impressions

The first image that we have of God—big G O D—is our dads. That's our first inkling of a higher power and it's the first association that we make with God. And how daddy is, is directly related to what we think God is like when we're one and two and three and four years old. But daddies aren't perfect. Some dads are *real* imperfect. Some dads are abusive, neglectful, drunks, cheating on momma—they're gone, they're workaholics, they're rigid, they're...lots of things. Some dads aren't portraying a very good image of God. And that's the first image that we get.

Then, when we get old enough, momma may decide that we need to go to church because daddy's such a jerk. Then we get dragged down to church. To the First Baptist Church or the Catholic Church or the First Christian Church or the Church of Christ—whatever church—just a church. We're thrown into our little Sunday School class, and they start talking to us about Jesus. We learn some stories, and those are kinda neat; and then we go to the service, and that's sort of interesting; and then we start getting printed with religion, dogma and doctrine, interpretation of scripture, and what this relationship is that we are supposed to have with God. But we don't know, at that point, whether we even have a relationship with God or not. Some of us do, some of us don't.

Then we move through that era of our life that I call the age of reason, when we begin to make decisions for ourselves. We may go to a church that we choose and we like it and we get free. We go down front, accept Christ, get prayed for, and Jesus frees us from lots of things. We get immediate deliverance from some things.

Then the work starts—the walk starts. We begin to read the Bible and issues begin to come up. When we approach God, we drag with us daddy and all the religious baggage that we've brought with us.

Then we're praying and talking to God about things like the second step and the sixth step. We say something like, "I now have this relationship with You. I want to improve on this relationship with You. I figured out at least three things that I do believe about You. And I got about five hundred things hanging on me here and I don't know whether I believe them or not. I don't know if they're the truth. I don't know whether they came from You, or from my dad, from Sunday school, from the preacher, or from...I don't know where."

So when we look at God, we have to look at Him through all that baggage.

Clear the tunnel

So, the second step and sixth step continue the process of clearing out the avenue or the tunnel between us and God the Father through Jesus. It's a continuation of the improvement of the personal relationship with God by *removing...removing* the things that are a lie.

When we get over into religion and law and these things, we do it backward. Instead of going in and removing this stuff, we go to a new church and they add some more to it. We get a new "honey-do" list. "Honey, if you'll do this and act like that and walk like this and dress like that and talk like this and be like that...*then* God will be okay with you, you'll be okay with Him. Everything will be all right."

They might say, "Now I know you're saved by grace, and everything's all right—*but...but* you need to join this group, you need to pay that, you need to believe this, you need to do this, act this way and don't act that way—" down the line. And, *if* we want the approval of our new daddy, represented by the pastor of whatever church it is and his connection to Big Daddy, then we'll do these do's. And if we don't—I don't know—gonna have a little trouble with the connection.

Religious abuse

Religious abuse is the imprinting of a works mentality, a doctrine, or dogma on someone as conditional to receiving the love of God. It doesn't come from any specific religion—it can come from any religion, or it can come from a person who is religiously rigid.

The receiver of abuse and religious manipulation is one who accepts the conditions that they've been told they have to fulfill in order to be acceptable, in order to be who they need to be in Christ.

There are also control issues and power struggles within religious structures. The people, their abilities, their money, and their commitments are used to further the ends or the agenda of the person or persons in authority.

I think that religious abuse and religious printing is at the very core of what keeps us from moving further in our relationship with God as we seek deliverance from these defects of character. Without addressing that issue, it's impossible for us to move past a certain place because we continue to drag that baggage with us. Whenever we think about God, we think about God through those erroneous ideas or erroneous religious printings that we have.

We alcoholics, drug addicts, sexaholics, workaholics, codependents are shame-based people. We're trying to achieve some feeling of being okay, but if we're carrying the religious abuse with us all the time, we never achieve that—we're powerless to live up to the standard. So our failure just triggers more shame and the shame triggers whatever we medicate our shame with.

A tremendous amount of shame can come out of religion. We're told from the beginning that we live under sin under the Adamic man until we are delivered from that by Jesus, but how much works mentality has been heaped on us and how much shame we bring to that experience with Jesus is directly relative to how free we are able to get by becoming born again.

Religious abuse is the major block that keeps people from returning to Jesus, or returning to church, or returning to any kind of a religious application of spirituality in their life that is Christ-centered because, in their minds, Christ equals all this abuse. When we bring up Jesus, we bring up all this religiosity; and it's not that people don't want Jesus, it's that they don't want the abuse that came with the guy that brought Jesus to them.

Drop the baggage

So this is what needs to happen: We need to come in, list out what the baggage is, and begin to throw it away. Throw it out. Get rid of it. Drop it. Take it off. Dump it.

Then what happens, *if* we have had a genuine acceptance of Jesus Christ into our hearts and the Holy Spirit dwells in our hearts and God Almighty lives in our spirits, is that we will *automatically* become who we are in Christ Jesus.

You are powerless and I am powerless to become like Jesus. I cannot add one hair to my head and I cannot do *one thing* to be more like Jesus except to let go of the junk that I drag with me and let *Him* become who He is in me.

The sixth step is about being willing to let go of some more stuff. It's like having the light in us and putting a bushel basket over it, just as the scripture says.[3] It's the lifting off of the basket and all that's covering up the Spirit of God.

Step Six is important

Step Six, like Step Two, is another one of those steps that we read and, at first glance, we think, "Why do we need to do this? Let's just get to it." But it's a key step in the second half of these twelve principles. Just like the clergyman said, "It separates the men from the boys." That's because anybody who is willing to actually have a relationship with God, and on a daily basis pick up his cross and walk it out, is truly coming into the wholeness of Jesus Christ.

---

[3]Matthew 5:15

—— **STEP SIX - ACTION** ——

You have now completed your inventory and shared that with God and with another person. In this process you were able to identify resentments that you have toward persons, institutions, or principles. This led you to realize that there are people in your life to whom you owe amends. You also discovered defects of your own character in the process. Now you are ready to take Step Six. Meditate on the step before answering the following questions.

**Were entirely ready to have God remove
all these defects of character.**

The purpose of this step is to bring you to a willingness to take that list of character defects to God. The actual step of asking Him to remove them comes in the next step.

A. *Taking Action*

In these lectures, defects of character have been described as "baggage." Religious abuse was identified as one of the significant "bags" we carry around, and it may be at the core of many of our behavioral responses. Believing this is the case, you need to consider the following questions:

1. In what ways have you experienced religious abuse?

2. How have these affected what you believe about God?

3. How have you experienced religion more than relationship with God?

4. What are some times you've experienced God's presence?

5. What did it make you feel when you experienced His presence?

6. Do you believe God wants a relationship with *you?*

7. Are you willing for God to reach out to you?

8. Do you want a closer relationship with God?   If not, why not?

9. What things do you think hinder that closer relationship from happening? Do you feel unworthy? Fearful? Doubtful?

10. What defects are you enjoying so much that you are unwilling to let go of them at the present time?

11. Review the consequences that you listed in Step Four. Have any of those consequences resulted from the defects that you are unwilling to have removed?

12. Are there consequences of having those defects that you are unwilling to have removed that you have not listed? What are they?

Pray for the willingness to let go of these defects.

13. What can you do about those things that hinder you from having a closer relationship with God?

14. What do you think God can do about those things?

15. Are you willing for God to do what He can to remove those hindrances, defects, etc.?

16. Are you willing to be made willing for God to take away these hindrances?

17. Do you believe the removal of these hindrances would improve your relationship with God?

18. Are you now ready to take the step and pray the prayer?   If not, why not?

B. *In your journal:*
1. What things have you noticed about taking this step as it relates to all the aspects of your life?
2. In what ways have you discovered God or sensed his presence in your life?
3. What victories have you had?
4. What defeats have you had?

Humbly asked Him to remove our shortcomings.

Humility

Since Step Seven says, *"Humbly* asked Him to remove our shortcomings," I want to deal with humility first. I'll begin by explaining what it is not.

Humiliation

We have all experienced *humiliation,* which has to do with being embarrassed. Most of us—because of our upbringing, our low self-worth, or the shame-based guilt feelings that we are still carrying—are real familiar with humiliation. It comes from not being able to perform according to whatever perfectionistic ideas that we have, or whatever perfectionistic expectations that were put on us as children by our parents, or by the perfectionistic expectations of an employer, a girlfriend or boyfriend. But this is not the same thing as humility.

False humility

There's also something we sometimes think is humility, but is really *false humility,* or what I call "reverse pride." It's the one that I call "rolling your hat brim." Somebody comes in all hunched over, head hanging, and they're rolling that hat brim. It's a manipulation. It's just another form of pride.

One of the best lessons about false humility that I've ever gotten came many years ago. After a support group meeting, an older lady came up to me and said, "Mike, those are nice shoes you've got on."

As she started to walk off, I said, "Oh, these old shoes? Why someone *gave* me these shoes. I've been wearing them for quite a while, and I just polished them up a little bit, and they've even got holes in them, but...gosh, it was nice of you to say that."

125

So, she turned to me and said (she was kind of a crusty old gal), "O'Neil, I'm going to pray for you, and I'm going to pray that you'll stay in this process long enough to just say, 'Thank you.'" And then she turned around and walked off. It took me about three weeks to figure out what she had said to me because I was still in a pretty heavy fog, but it finally dawned on me.

Examine yourself and think about those times when someone has come up to you and said, "Boy, you sang a great song! I really enjoyed that. I was really blessed by that!" (Or whatever they've said to you.)

And you said, "Oh, me...it wasn't really anything..." And inside you're going, "Man, I can't get a record deal, can't get a gig, or can't get..." But on the outside you've got that "Oh, I'm so humble...It's just a gift from God."

That's generally the kind of humility that we walk in. Why? Because, basically, we're all egomaniacs with an inferiority complex. We get mad at somebody for not noticing us—how talented we are, how wonderful we are, how giving we are, what a great person we are. "I'm a great speaker but they don't recognize me at that church. They oughta have *me* up there..." And then when somebody does come to us, we go into our phoney baloney inferiority complex—"Who? Oh, me? I'm not sure I could do that." It's egomania with an inferiority complex.

That's one of the defects or behavior patterns that the seventh step is going to address. Hopefully, by the time we've reached this step, we're in touch with that and already have that on our fourth step list.

True humility

So, how do we define humility?

Most of us read some attributes or virtues about humility and decide we need to be humble. We wake up the next morning, and since we've been such a jerk yesterday with somebody, we decide, "I'm going to be humble today. Yesterday I was a jerk, but today I'll be humble." So we go out and we try to practice being humble. And that doesn't work either. We cannot do that. We are powerless to be humble. In our human condition, we cannot effect humility in our walk.

True humility has to be a by-product of breaking through the denial, being in that relationship with God, dying to self.

Humility is recognizing the truth about ourselves, both the positive things and the negative things. If we stay in the truth about ourselves everyday, then we'll stay in humility. To Christianize it, if we stay in the knowledge and awareness of who we are in Christ Jesus and who we were in the flesh, the by-product of that thought process will be humility, ongoing humility. It's impossible to get proud when we can take absolutely no credit for anything other than raising our hands and saying, "Yes, I will."

Repentance

We've been told to repent, or change our thinking. (The word "repent" in the Bible comes from the Greek word *metanoia—meta,* change; and *noia,* mind or reason). Repentance has to become a way of life. But we go down front and pray, or we kneel down by ourselves, and we decide to repent—and then we go out and do exactly the same thing over and over again. We might last for a day or a week or maybe longer.

Steps Four through Nine walk us through repentance. First, we own who we are and the problem. We ask, "What do I need to repent from?" And that breaks through the denial. Then we get in touch with the fact that we can't do anything about it. So we go *humbly* before God and ask Him to do something about it. *Then* comes a change in the way that we act and react in relationships with other people. He wants us to have a relationship with Him above all relationships, then He wants that relationship to be our basis for all other relationships.

Later, in Steps Eight and Nine, we go to other people and make amends in order to keep the tunnel clear between us and God. We change how we relate to them. So we change our thinking.

Otherwise, we think, "I resent her and I'm not going to make amends to her. I resent her, I want to resent her, I deserve to resent her, and I can feel sorry for myself if I keep resenting her. That's the way it is. She owes me money. I don't want to go ask her for money—I just want to resent her."

Go to her, make peace, and God will change the way you think about her, and God will change the way you behave in that relationship. That's repentance. God grants repentance.[1]

So, humility is a by-product of a relationship with Jesus Christ in the death to self and our resurrection in Him by the Spirit. The extent to which the reality of His death and resurrection is walked out through us during each day, is the extent to which we have true humility. And the very instant that we're walking that out and we think, "My, that was humble," we just lost it. If we claim it for ourselves, we've just lost it.

It's like the man who was given an award for humility. When he displayed it, they took it away from him.

Grieving

I'll come back to humility later, but I want to talk now about an interesting aspect of Step Seven called "grieving."

This "grieving" was revealed to me one time when another fellow and I were taking the Twelve Steps. We had done Step One for a week, then Step Two for a week, then Step Three for a week. We had written Four, and it had taken about three weeks for us to take Step Five. We had just recently done Six, and then we were up to Seven. We had shared our fourth steps with each other, we were holding ourselves accountable, and God was really working.

Then we got down to the week for the seventh step. We kept our

---

[1] 2 Timothy 2:25

journals every week about what was going on with us concerning each step. Then we would meet on Sunday nights and we would share our journals— "Here's how I saw God on this step, and here's what's going on." The process was really working. On the seventh step as we shared our journals we noticed that we were more depressed than at any other time. We couldn't explain it.

We were flat. We just kinda went through our daily work—just hung our heads and did our thing. So we got to Sunday night and we were sharing with each other.

"You know, I felt kinda down this week, kinda flat—I don't know, just kinda blah. How are you feeling?"

"Well, I feel about the same way."

And we started asking, "Well, what's going on? Why do we feel like this? We took the first three steps, and, man, we were on fire for God. It was rough getting through Four and Five—writing that stuff and really sharing everything about ourselves for our whole life—but I really felt deliverance and my load lightened after Step Five. Why do we feel depressed?"

We talked about it for a while. We had our defect list there because we were going to pray the seventh step prayer about removing them. So we discussed it for a while and we came to this conclusion: We were grieving. We were grieving at the loss that was about to occur and was occurring in our lives—the loss of the defects.

Losing the defects

We don't want to lose these defects, these patterns of behavior, even though they're destructive and have been holding us in bondage our whole lives—even killing us. If it's alcohol or drugs, it's killing us even faster than some of the other things. These things are harming other people, too. Even though we're sick and tired of them, we're used to them. They're familiar old pals, and we know how they work. We can rely on a certain destructive behavior to produce specific results and often produce our payoff—self-pity.

We discovered that we were grieving over the prospect of losing all these character defects and patterns of behaviors. These had been the tools that we used in our lives to justify our emotion or feeling of choice. When we examined ourselves, we found that, more than anything else, we wanted to feel sorry for ourselves. After all was said and done, no matter what else had happened, we had an overwhelming drive inside of us to feel sorry for ourselves.

A revelation

Finding out that self-pity was the driving force behind why I did things was a great revelation. I discovered that I found people who had done things to me unjustly so that I could resent them, so that I could feel sorry for myself and be a victim. If I had a positive situation happen in my life, I would turn it around in my mind so that I became a martyr, or turn it around so it didn't work out and I could feel sorry for myself. I found out that self-pity was my emotion of choice. Fear, anger, and everything else always led me back to self-pity.

Self-pity is what Satan used on Adam and Eve to con them into sinning. "Don't you feel sorry for yourself because you're not like God? You can be like God, man, if you'd do this over here. He's God and He's got the best deal. You're getting the short end of the stick, but if you'll come over here and eat..." (And then they ate the fruit, got kicked out of the garden, and then *really* had a reason to feel sorry for themselves.)

Everything we do in our human condition is destined to set us up for self-pity. Pride goes before the fall, but what really opens the door to Satan is self-pity. The minute we open that self-pity door, a voice comes in and justifies all kinds of behavior:

"My wife doesn't sleep with me, and, you know, I've got needs."

"My boss doesn't really pay me what I deserve; so, I'll take home a few pounds of copper every night from the plant and sell it over the fence."

"My kids don't act the way I think they ought to act, and I'm such a great parent—worked so hard all these years to do things right. It just isn't worth it. I might as well go get drunk."

We forget about the consequences—we just wallow in self-pity.

So as my friend and I looked back through the first six steps, we discovered that we could, because of our obsessive-compulsive, destructive behavior patterns, take any situation, no matter how good the situation, and turn it into a reason to feel sorry for ourselves. Not only *could* we do that, but we *had* done that.

So here we were at the seventh step, and it was all laid out in front of us in black and white, written, staring at us. And there we were, right on that paper. We had spent one week trying to be humble enough to let God remove these defects and trying to be willing to have that done. But we knew, since He had done everything that He had said He would do up through Step Six, that He was probably going to do this, too, and we were going to lose the mother-lode deal of how we had been our whole lives. These defects were the ultimate form of idolatry—wanting them instead of God.

We couldn't believe what we had discovered. Both of us looked at each other at the same time, and we said, "My God. Can you believe that we are that sick?"

Well, that opened the door for us to be able to approach God in a new way, with new knowledge and new understanding about ourselves, and to come into His presence as we had through the first six steps—and once again it threw us all the way back to the beginning, to Step One, to our lack of power.

Powerless

I had thought I was gaining on this deal by now, you know? But I was powerless not only over the defects that were on the paper, I was powerless over the desire to give them up—and I had just discovered a new reason for wanting to keep them, and I was powerless over that, too. I had to come to believe that God could give me the willingness to let go of them, turn that over to Him, and then believe that He could get me through the grieving process when all those things began to leave me. So that's what we did.

We got our lists out and followed the old recommended way to do this step. We got *on our knees* and humbly asked God to remove our defects of character.

Taking the step

When we get ready to take this step, we need three things: us, another person, and the paper with those defects, resentments, and amends. We get with this other person, kneel down and say, out loud, this seventh step prayer.

"Father, I come to You as I am and ask You to change me, to remove from me these defects of character. I'm now willing for You to reshape me in Your image. Remove my resentments, take away the hate in my heart for my fellow man, give me the willingness and strength to move forward to make amends. Clear a path in my spirit, my soul, and my mind that Your Spirit might flow through and in me and cut these things out of me with Your sword of truth and Your word. May Your Spirit rise up in me. Help me to let my old self die that I might live in the newness of Your life. In Jesus name, Amen."

Then, out loud, using our list, we read about the specific **resentments** and ask God to help us with those. If there are people or things that we don't want to quit hating, we ask Him to give us the willingness to stop hating them.

We're getting ready to face these and other people to make **amends** in Steps Eight and Nine. We ask God to remove the self-centered defects that block us from being willing to proceed with making those amends.

Then we get the mother-lode **defect** list out, and we start down that list—self-pity, pride, lust, greed, perfectionism, etc. (And if you've done your work well, it's a fairly long list.) We pray, out loud, for God to remove these defects and replace them with those attributes that He would have us to have.

If it's self-pity (that's just self-centeredness), we ask Him to make us other-centered, God-centered. We ask him to replace pride with humility. To give us God's love instead of lust. Generosity or charity instead of greed. Make us understanding instead of perfectionistic. And so on and so forth.

Here's a list I've used in the past. Perhaps it will help you.

Defect	Replace with	Defect	Replace with
self-pitying	God/other-centeredness	smug	open-minded
prideful, arrogant	humble	panicky, violent	stable
lustful	God's love (*agape*)	stubborn	gracious
greed	generosity, charity	inconsistent	consistent
perfectionistic	understanding	envious	content
self-centered	awareness of others	discourteous	courteous
self-indulgent	helpful to others	unkind	kind
selfish	generous	indifferent	loving, caring
domineering	cooperative	lacking discretion	discreet
judgmental	constructively critical	insincere	sincere
impatient	patient	dishonest	honest
intolerant	tolerant	ungrateful	thankful
unrealistic	realistic	lazy	industrious
unreasonable	reasonable	withdrawn	outgoing
aimless	purposeful	worrisome	calm
irresponsible	responsible	tense	relaxed
resentful, angry	forgiving	fearful, apprehensive	confident, having faith
suspicious	trusting	despondent	hopeful
prone to gossip	trustworthy	disagreeable	agreeable
pessimistic	optimistic	living in the past	living for today
depressed	cheerful	insecurity	trust in God
rigidity	spontaneity	self-righteous	willing to admit faults
procrastinating	prompt		
disinterested in self	using talents and abilities		
complacent	willing to seek emotion and spiritual balance		

If you have trouble with the opposites to your list, go to the scriptures. If there is an index or references in the back of your Bible, it will help you find these. Look for the remedy. Hunt them down.

Motives

God takes and works bad things for His good. That means, for example, that if you're a controlling person, you might become a good leader or a good manager. God can take that negative thing and turn it around—turn it inside out and make it a positive thing—make you a good manager or a good leader by changing the motive.

You see, most of the time, the things on our list are negatives instead of positives because of our **motive**. That's always what's wrong. If our motives are in line with God's will, then whatever we're doing and however we're being will be fine. When we move from God-centered to self-centered, self-serving, self-pitying, self-whatever, and our motives move from God to self in some form, then we end up in those defects and destructive patterns.

And beware—we are masters at rationalizing how to twist and turn and massage that motive so that it looks like, "I'm a benevolent, kind, considerate, person" when all the time I'm trying to manipulate this person over here to sign me to his publishing company or give me a job or go out on a date with me or give me two dollars or be my friend or paint my house. *Motives.*

So we examine ourselves. As we're coming down through these steps and splitting ourselves open, we're looking around inside—we're getting in touch with what our motives are. What is actually driving our lives— driving our bus? Why do I do what I do? "Well, it's because my dad beat me." Yeah, okay. What motive are you left with and how are you using that as an excuse to go beat your kid? Those kind of things. Look for the motive.

From God or Self?

Is it God? Or is it self? Only two masters to serve: God or self.

Motive from God?
Motive from Self?
to do what I do

God or *self*. Satan operates in self. That's where he gets you. He's got an easy job with most of us, because he just goes down this list and says, "Well, let me see. What's the easiest way we can get O'Neil to feel sorry for himself? Mmmm—let's get funny with his money. That gets him every time."

Almost everything on my defect list that comes into my life to attack me has the tendency to cause my old man nature to rise up.

This happened and that happened and that happened…and I need to feel sorry for myself. That's when I have to go, "Wait a minute. Hold it. I have a choice. Now that I'm a born-again Christian, a new creation in Christ, I now have a choice."

I didn't used to have a choice. I just took it—"Oh, yeah? Self-pity? Okay, thank you very much." Now I have a choice. I can say, "No, I renounce that. I'm not going to feel sorry for myself. I know God has some reason for my money to get funny. He may be trying to get my attention— trying to correct me in an area of spending, or even possibly letting me know that I've become idolatrous with finances and that I need to continually look to Him as my source. But all I know is that God's in charge of my life." So, I ask God to remove me from self-pity: "Don't let me wallow in self-pity."

Self-pity

In my little house that I live in with my lovely wife and my lovely children, it's a contest to see who can feel sorry for themselves the fastest, the longest, and get away with it without the rest of them catching you. Everybody is so good at it and so aware of it. I'll be on the couch, head down, sour look, and one of my kids will walk through. Momma, in the other room, will say, "Where's Dad?"

"Ah, he's over on the couch feeling sorry for himself."

The kid just walked in the door. He hasn't even spoken to me yet, but he just knows the look.

Sometimes when self-pity comes up, I want to go with it—"I've a choice here, and I'm choosing self-pity. I just want to feel sorry for myself. I just want to feel rotten for awhile. So, I'll just go over there and I'll do that."

And people will try to help: "Why don't you think about this and why don't you do that and, here, let's pray." I don't want to pray, I don't want to be ministered to, I don't want to talk to you, I don't want to call anybody, I don't want to hear about God, I don't want to hear any positive stuff—"Well, count your blessings"—I don't want to hear about my blessings. I want to burn 'em all down...so I'll have some more stuff to feel sorry for myself about.

Sometimes I just have to sit there until I'm through—because I can't let go of it. I just do. And then, I get tired of feeling sorry for myself, especially in my house, where you can't get *any*body to feel sorry for you with you—nobody.

Back to humility

Now I want to go back to humility.

We're ready to take Step Seven. We pray our prayer, we ask for these things to be removed, and we get in touch with "how sick we are." Believe me, when we get in touch with how sick we really are in our human condition, it is an extremely humbling experience.

Humility, therefore, comes about as a by-product of God's process of recovery and sanctification through these steps. And like I said earlier, if you recognize it and try to do it, you lose it. It's going on when you don't know anything about it. God is walking out His life through you, and you're dying to self, and you're unaware of yourself...and you're unaware of the humility.

Are you ready now to take the step? Or do you need to go back to Step Six?

——— STEP SEVEN · ACTION ———

In Steps Four through Seven you are in the process of making peace with yourself. You made that searching inventory, admitted the exact nature of your wrongs, and have become entirely ready for God to remove all these defects of character. Now, in this step, you are going to actually get down on your knees and ask God to remove them.

Meditate on this step for a moment before continuing the action.

Humbly asked Him to remove our shortcomings.

The purpose of this step is to bring those defects of character to God without reservations and ask Him to remove them.

A. *Taking Action*
  1. Before praying answer these questions:
    a. What things about true humility have you experienced so far?

    b. In order to take Step Seven, you need to have a humble and contrite heart—breaking through pride. Do you sense that you now have that?

    c. Are you truly willing to let it all go and let God take all of it?

    d. If you're not, what are you not yet willing to let go of?

    e. Is your list of defects, amends, and resentments thorough and honest? Make sure it is thorough and honest before you take the step.

  2. With at least one other person, get on your knees and pray this Step Seven prayer as sincerely as you can:

"Father, I come to You as I am and ask You to change me, to remove from me these defects of character. I'm now willing that You reshape me in Your image. Remove my resentments, take away the hate in my heart for my fellow man, give me the willingness and strength to move forward to make amends. Clear a path in my spirit, my soul, and my mind that Your Spirit might flow through and in me and cut these things out of me with Your sword of truth and Your word. May Your Spirit rise up in me. Help me to let my old self die that I might live in the newness of Your life. In Jesus name, Amen."

3. *Defects:* Now ask God to remove each specific defect and replace it with His attributes. (See the listing in the lecture or use a Bible index and references to help you determine these.) For example, pray, "Lord, remove pride, and replace it with humility."

4. *Resentments:* Go back to your list of resentments in Step Four and pray, "Dear Lord, I now ask you to help me overcome my resentments and unforgiveness toward those who have harmed me, or those whom I perceived have harmed me."

If you're still unwilling to forgive anyone, then pray, "Lord, make me willing to stop resenting and willing to forgive _____."

Next, say out loud (and repeat the statement for each person you are forgiving), "I forgive you, _____."

5. *Amends:* Finally, ask the Lord to give you the strength to ask forgiveness from and make amends to each one on your amends list.

6. If you're in a support group, allow time for each one to pray through his/her own list.

B. *In your journal:*
1. What things have you noticed about taking this step as it relates to all the aspects of your life?
2. In what ways have you discovered God or sensed His presence in your life?
3. What victories have you had?
4. What defeats have you had?

STEP EIGHT

**Made a list of all persons we had harmed
and became willing to make amends to them all.**

By the time we finished Step Four (the moral inventory) and Step Five (admitting it to somebody), we had a list of amends. When we get to Step Eight, there may be a need for us to increase that list, depending on how thoroughly we did Steps Four, Five, Six, and Seven. We may find someone or something we need to add.

The goal of Step Eight is to complete the list and then become "willing to the list." That's the essence of the step—to become willing to make the amends. We have the list of people we've harmed—and we just spend some time being willing to make amends to them for the harm that we've done them.

Selfishness

What constitutes harm? Usually, **selfishness**.

Here's a very important quote from the book *Alcoholics Anonymous* regarding Self:

"Selfishness—self-centeredness! That, we think, is the root of our troubles. Driven by a hundred forms of fear, self-delusion, self-seeking, and self-pity, we step on the toes of our fellows and they retaliate. Sometimes they hurt us, seemingly without provocation, but we invariably find that at some time in the past we have made decisions based on self which later placed us in a position to be hurt."[1]

The key is in the last line, *"We have made decisions based on self which later placed us in a position to be hurt"* by others. That's why some of

---

[1]*Alcoholics Anonymous*, p. 62.

the people who are on our amends list are also on our resentment list.

We think the reason we do destructive things is because people do all those things to *us,* and it's *their* fault, and if they wouldn't be that way, then we wouldn't act this way. We have to take that and reverse it—look at the self-centered side of it—examine it and look for *our* selfishness. Look at the times we've made decisions based on selfishness which have placed us in a position to be harmed by others. I find that people don't do things to us; people just do things, and we react to them.

So, many of those we've harmed, we also resent. It takes **forgiveness** to overcome resentments. In other words, we have to forgive and come to be at peace with others. That's one of the things that this step is about.

People we have harmed

As we examined ourselves in our self-centered decisions through Steps Four and Five, we found that we had harmed people. When we read to another person about our resentments, our feelings, our past, and all the things that we wrote in Step Four, hopefully, that person helped us to realize who those people are.

We want to be at peace with others, not get them to be at peace with us, but we generally turn it around. Examine your list and see if you've put somebody on there whom you just want to be at peace with you, or want them to like you—but you haven't harmed them. You have to define "harm." Have *I harmed* this person?

There could be some guy or some gal who just doesn't like you, and he or she has a right to that. "For some reason, Maybelle just doesn't like me. I've done everything I can do to get her to like me. Now that I've come to this amends list, I think I'll put her name on there and go make some amends to Maybelle." But we haven't harmed Maybelle. Making amends to her would be yet another self-centered manipulation.

Because of our own low self-esteem and low self-worth, we want Maybelle to like us. So we go over there and say, "Maybelle, will you get at peace with me?" That's the opposite of what we're doing here.

We're responsible for what we think of other people, but *it's none of our business what others think of us.* That's a concept that was very difficult for me as a codependent ACOA (adult child of an alcoholic) to grasp. My human condition tells me that I need your approval—I need you to like me and accept me because that's where I get my self-worth (instead of getting it from a relationship with God). So, I'll do anything to get you to accept me and like me and approve of me.

(And there was a time, if I couldn't get you to like me, that I would assassinate your character and plot your demise—so that I could justify my own existence and try to feel better about myself.)

So, make sure your list includes people that you really have harmed. If we've really *harmed* Maybelle, we need to get at peace with her. But she can stay mad at us. Hopefully, she won't. Hopefully, making amends will fix this. If we continue this process and continue to walk out God's life in our life, maybe Maybelle will heal. But she'll never heal without our forgiving her. We need to get *us* at peace with her.

Shame

Shame and all the hidden feelings in the shame corral play a part in the **self-centered syndrome** that constitutes the harm that we cause others. This syndrome abounds in dysfunctional families.

Dysfunctional families

If you grew up in a dysfunctional family, you had rules. Some were unspoken rules, and your family would have been in denial about having those rules. Nevertheless, you had them. You didn't consciously think about the rules until it came time to obey one, and then you just obeyed it.

Some basic rules are don't talk, don't feel, don't trust, don't share, keep secrets.

The no-talking rule prohibits anybody talking about a feeling. "We don't talk about our feelings." In an alcoholic home, Dad's there, angry, or passed out at the dinner table, and the family sits around and just goes, "May I have some more potatoes?"

(There's a commercial that one of the treatment centers had that was a favorite of mine. It was the one with the elephant. The family was sitting around the house watching television, and the elephant was the alcoholic. They literally took a house and an elephant and made this elephant walk through the house. He totally destroyed the house—just smacked everything—walked through the walls, knocked everything over, tore everything down—and the family just sits right on that couch and watches television the whole time. And the commercial said, "If you have an alcoholic in your home...")

Another rule is to be who the dysfunctional family says you need to be as opposed to who you really are, and that causes you not to know who you really are or to deny who you are. You create a false self and that false self is who interacts with your dysfunctional family. You also let that false self interact with the rest of the world. That's how you survive the dysfunction.

In other families the rules may be no touching, no hugging, don't show your feelings, remain distant, and mind your own business.

Another one is don't make mistakes. Mistakes are not okay. Mistakes come from imperfect humans, and you must be a perfect human to be in this family. With this rule you must shift the blame—whenever things don't turn out right, it's someone else's fault. In a dysfunctional family you can't be vulnerable.

There are double messages in dysfunctional families. A radical example is when Dad gets drunk, comes home, and screams at everybody or hits somebody. The next day he doesn't remember it at all, but the whole family is still reeling from it. He shows up at the breakfast table and says, "How about that football game last night? Boy, wasn't that great?" Or he really enjoyed this or that and "it's good to see you." Well, it wasn't good seeing him.

And there are double standards in dysfunctional families. A classic for the alcoholic is when the alcoholic is drinking but telling his kid not to smoke pot—"You stay off drugs!" Or maybe Dad isn't alcoholic; he just drinks beer but he tells the kid not to do drugs, socially or otherwise. Yet alcohol is a drug.

These rules and messages cause all sorts of feelings, but there's also the rule about not feeling. That rule causes all the feelings to be stuffed in the shame corral that we talked about in Step Four. We're not allowed to have feelings and not allowed to show feelings, so we're ashamed when those feelings come up. Feelings are bad, so they're not reflected or mirrored by the parents. Those feelings are not okay, so we have to do something. That's when we stuff them in the shame corral.

And remember that the parent doesn't have to be an alcoholic for all these rules to come up. It could be a religious addiction, or a strict upbringing, or a severe militaristic background in the home, or maybe the parents are just passing along the rules they had in their dysfunctional families growing up.

Destructive shame

Normal shame, or guilt, is something that we all have. Shame or guilt is experienced through our conscience. It's a gauge to tell us that we're doing something wrong. There's nothing wrong with that. Hopefully we can get back to having that in a normal way so that it can be a guide for us through life—to keep us honest.

But when normal shame becomes destructive shame because of a dysfunctional family upbringing, it becomes toxic shame. It's wrong and it's destructive because it changes from the message of "I'm guilty because of an act that I need to feel guilty about," or "I *made* a mistake," to "I'm defective, I *am* a mistake." No matter what I do, I'm just a mistake. That feeds low self-worth, low self-esteem and impairs the growth of the person into the full development and expression of who they really are.

That healthy feeling of shame is lost. The destructive shame takes over and controls those frozen feelings inside. That's what happens to us in the dysfunctional family.

A false self

As we come up out of our dysfunctional family, we assume a family role. It might be the role of a hero, or a scapegoat, or a lost child, or a mascot, or some other role, or a combination of all of those. The destructive shame produces that false self.

I detach from who I am on the inside, and I produce a false self that cannot have an intimate relationship with others. So, no matter what is going on or what I'm doing, because I'm out of touch with who I really am,

I fabricate this shell, this imitation of who I am, and that false self is who I use to relate to others. Therefore, it's impossible for shame-based people to acquire or achieve intimacy with other people.

Toxic shame blocks intimacy—men with men, men with women, women with women. Because who I really am is hidden away in the shame corral. But I manufactured this guy over here, this human doing instead of this human being, and he's the one who is having these relationships on the outside. When you start to get too close, the intimacy threatens to expose what's in the shame corral.

Do you remember that I talked about building up the shame through the years? —so that every feeling and emotion that I have is bound up in the corral, whether it's bad feelings, good feelings, joy, anger—whatever they are. All of our feelings are in here. They're all bound up in the shame corral.

So when we go out to have a relationship, we take this human doing person who's on the outside, and we enter into a relationship. When the relationship becomes intimate or the opportunity to be intimate avails itself, it starts poking on this corral, and when it pokes on this bag of feelings in there, **shame** rares its head with it's big whip and spanks all those feelings and goes, "You know you're not supposed to feel that. You don't deserve to feel that way and to be that way. You're a mistake. All those feelings are mistakes, too. You learned that! Now you put a smile on that face, boy, and you enter into that relationship, and you talk right and you act right with him or her."

That's some of what toxic shame tells us.

And then, as we move through life, we shame-based people seek out other shame-based people to have relationships with. Now we have two people like this and they get together and they get married. They're married for five years, or ten years, and then they come to see me for counseling. And they say, "I don't know what's going on in our marriage...it's been that way for years...I mean, he's just the way he is...she's just the way she is...sex has gone out of the marriage...he does his thing...she does her thing...everything's just flat."

And when I begin to inquire and dig into what's going on, we generally have an abused or neglected male—a son abused by his father who beat him or shamed him in some way. And the wife will be a shame-based female. And the two of them have been in this phoney-baloney relationship for five or ten years. Neither one of them is able to give their real selves to the other or to feel what they feel because they are not in touch with who they really are. It's extremely difficult to break down all those barriers. It's extremely difficult to get those two people to really give themselves permission to be intimate.

Male intimacy

Men are the worst with this, especially with other men. I have a real personal heart for men and intimate relationships with other men. And I'm not talking about hanging out with the guys in the sense of "Let's get our guns and our cigars and a six-pack of beer, and we'll cuss and shoot some ducks. We'll really get tight." That's not what I'm talking about. And don't misunderstand me, I'm not talking about homosexuality, either.

What I'm talking about is men trying to be intimate with other men. This is probably, in my opinion, the most widespread dysfunction in the body of Christ and in society at large. Men don't know how to be intimate with men because they never learned how to be intimate with their fathers. Now that's not true for everybody, because everybody's father didn't withhold love and affection, or neglect or abuse their sons in some way.

Nevertheless, many men have not had intimacy with their fathers, and they've been brought up to hide their feelings. (You know, men don't cry.) They continue to get messages as they grow up about not feeling and not showing feelings, so they don't know how to have intimate relationships, especially with other men. What I would like to see is men being able to cry and hug and share intimately with other men and being real men among men. That's what it's about.

Control - Fear - Anger

Control is a major defense for shame. As I move through life as a shame-bound person, I have to maintain control.

As I said earlier, self-centeredness and a hundred forms of fear are at the core of our being, and that causes us to make decisions based on self. Those decisions put us in a position for others to appear to hurt us, when actually we are the ones causing the harm.

Those actions or those behaviors are directly tied to the fact that we are shame-based. The shame-based person is a self-centered person, even though that person appears to be laying down his life for humanity. All he can think about is himself. "How do I look, how do I feel, what's going on with me..."

In a men's group once, they were talking about going to a party and wanting to be the center of attention but being scared to death and wondering what everyone was going to think and should I talk or should I tell that joke or should I talk to this person or should I sit back—all that ruminating in the mind. That's all self-centered garbage. All of it is. "Oh, I don't want to go talk to that person—I might say something wrong and hurt their feelings." That's self-centered. It's just self-centered fear, and fear has us bound up.

Now fear ties into the shame corral. I begin to approach this corral, and I begin to open the door, but it's jam packed with feelings. They're all in there and they're just bustin' at the walls. When I crack that door, a lifetime of feelings begin to come forth and they're huge by now. So I'm

threatened by the prospect of having to look
at or talk about these feelings with you—
actually express them—it's just too scary
for me. I can't do it.

That just fires up more shame and
fear, and then I become even more self-
centered. Then I begin to feel guilty about
being self-centered, so I go into my
codependency and become a volunteer
victim—then I resent the person I've
martyred myself for and I ultimately get my payoff feeling of self-pity.
Then, almost always, the next emotion that comes out is anger. The anger
may be expressed in rage, or it may be passive-aggressive (smiling on the
outside but seething on the inside).[2] After it becomes anger, it'll transform
into one of my obsessive-compulsive behaviors—drinking, bingeing on food,
gambling, a sexual desire—whatever it takes to medicate the shame.

We're ashamed of feeling shame. Shame makes us feel bad, and we
want to feel good. So, we'll do something like get the credit card out and go
shopping.

(My personal thing is going to the warehouse store because it's real
cheap and I buy up batteries. You can always use batteries. So, when I get
off into my shame deal and self-pity and fear and feeling rotten and angry, I
get the wife and the kids and I get in the car, go down to the discount store,
and spend ten dollars—"Let's get some batteries! ...ahh, I feel so much
better." It's a way to medicate. I know it's kind of cheesy, but you take what
you can get.)

You see, healthy shame is lost in the frozen feelings that are in the
shame corral, so there's no way to operate in healthy shame. We're either
the human doing who is performing perfectly at the optimum out here, or
we're the worst slime of the earth. And with this syndrome working, we
can't change how we are. We can only change what we do.

Volunteer victim

Here's how the volunteer victim syndrome works.

We think we're sacrificing ourselves for others. We're told that we're
supposed to be other-centered, we're supposed to care about other people

---

[2]Passive-aggressive is like the wife, the husband, or the boss who comes in, hands you a paper,
and says, "I need you to do this."

And you say with a big smile on your face, "Sure. I'll get right to it. You bet." He or she
leaves, and you toss the paper ... right in the trash.

Instead of honestly saying, "I'm not doing that. That's not my job. You're always putting this
on my desk and I'm sick of it"—you say, "Yessir. No problem. Oh, thank you sooo much for
placing that in my responsibility." ... and in the trash it goes.

And when he comes back next week and says, "Where's that deal?"

You say, "Oh, darn. I'm sooo sorry. I forgot it somehow."

That's passive-aggressive.

and place their needs before our own—and those spiritual truths are in scripture and they are valid truths. However, if you're a shame-based person, full of toxic shame, you do those things out of the wrong motive. Those of us who live our lives making those sacrifices out of guilt and shame become victims—volunteer victims. But we don't realize we're setting ourselves up, and then we come up with resentments because we're the victim.

We spend our time being a victim for a while and then we become angry. Because we have a fear of conflict or confrontation, we avoid being assertive. Then after we get so angry we can't contain it, we become aggressive—we go in and scream at somebody or resent them. Then we feel guilty and bad, so we skip back over assertion again and move back into the victim role.

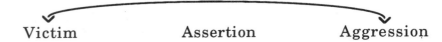

Victim   Assertion   Aggression

As volunteer victims we sacrifice ourselves, our own things, our own health, and our own well-being for others. That's not what being other-centered means. Charity begins at home. We have to be in some kind of shape ourselves to be any good to anybody else. But if we've lived from a place of shame, as those of us who came from dysfunctional families do, then we don't think we deserve God's forgiveness—we don't think we deserve anything that's good. But we think these other people do, and we think that if we do things for other people we can earn our way into being okay.

Still powerless

When the shame syndrome is in place and I'm feeling like slime, the preacher comes to me and tells me, "Okay, all you have to do is come and believe on this scripture that says you're a new creature in Christ. That's all you have to do." And he's right—that *really is* all I have to do. It really, really is. The problem is, I can't do that. I won't give myself permission to do that because of all that stuff inside my shame corral.

But I come and I *try* to do that, and everything that seems to be happening for everybody else at church isn't happening for me. I'm still buying hundreds of batteries at the discount store, or whatever it is I'm doing—drinking, the sex addiction, obsessive-compulsive eating, or feeling terrible.

Just feeling terrible and not medicating at all—that's a good one. Then we get suicidal. We decide we'll just end it all, and we can't figure out why. "Man, I believe the scriptures, I'm born again, I've been baptized in the Holy Ghost, I've been sprinkled, dipped, and dry-cleaned—the whole nine yards—I'm reading a hundred scriptures everyday, and I—I feel like a worm. What's the deal?"

The deal is that we can't get past this shame stuff until we begin to face it and be rid of it. Facing it has to do with forgiveness, amends, restitution, and peace with our past so that God can transform us in the present.

Now there are some folks who are sitting in the pews today—probably most of them, I don't know—who came to church and heard the scriptures about Jesus is Lord and "I'm a new creature" and all that, and they went down front, they got prayed for, they believed, they accepted it, "I forgive myself and God forgives me and I believe that," and they just went on. And they're doing fine. They don't have this problem. But I could never do it. I could watch those other people do it. I could watch them get victory over all kinds of things and watch them do all kinds of things. But I couldn't do it. And that made me feel *more shame.*

Remember our steps back there? My problem is that I can't do it. In and of myself, I'm powerless to believe the truth about myself that God has told me. So, once again, when I get to here, I gotta go back to Step One, admit that I'm powerless to do Step Eight, but I'm willing, then admit that I'm powerless over all this shame business. "God, I have no idea how you're going to unravel all this."

Forgiveness

God tells me that the key that unlocks this shame corral is *forgiveness.*

However, it's not always easy to forgive. For a woman who has been sexually abused from the age of six to twelve by her alcoholic father, it's a little bit hard to forgive that guy. For the male who's been physically abused by the father—literally beaten bloody and ashamed to go to school because of bruises (and I've worked with lots of men who have)—for them to forgive old dad is really hard.

"You need to forgive your dad! That's what you need to do!"

Well, he tries to forgive his dad, but he's so mad at him, he wants to kill him. But over there in the scriptures it says you gotta be at peace with everybody and you can't hold any grudges.

It gets even more complicated in the syndrome of sexual abuse or physical abuse, because the child somehow assumes the guilt role. The girl thinks she did something to cause dad to sexually abuse her. I've never seen it fail yet. I've never counseled one female that was sexually abused that didn't have the thought that she caused it somehow. She was a seven-year-old girl laying in bed, she was extremely seductive, and caused her father to come sexually abuse her—come on, man! That's ridiculous, but that's what the child thinks. And the boy who's been beaten half to death thinks, "Well, I'm just a bad person. I could never do anything right, and I deserved all those beatings."

In those situations, before we can get to forgiveness, we have to get those individuals in a place where they can give themselves permission to get mad. They need to realize and be able to say, "This *wasn't* my fault. I *didn't* cause this to happen. This guy *was* a jerk. I *am* angry."

But they think, "Oh, I can't feel angry because I'm guilty" and that

145

makes them feel ashamed. See how it just perpetuates itself and throws you back into the whole thing? So, in therapy we have to give them permission to feel the anger before they can work towards getting rid of the resentment and coming to forgiveness.

I had always heard, "You need to forgive this person. If you have a resentment, you need to pray for them, and you need to forgive them, and it'll go away."

I prayed for this person for five years. Daily. "God, I forgive this person, I forgive him, I forgive him. I pray for him..." At the end of five years, I was taking these steps and had recently taken the fourth and fifth steps when this person that I resented called on the telephone and said, "Hello, can I talk to so-and-so?"

Just the sound of this person's voice sent me into an absolute rage. I began screaming at this person, took the phone and threw it against the wall. And then I stopped myself and I thought, "What was that? What was *that?* I've been forgiving and praying for this person for five years."

I called my sponsor up and told him the deal and he said, "It's that hate."

I said, "What hate?"

He said, "The hate you've got for him."

"Man, I don't hate him, I've been forgiving him."

He said, "Yeah, you do, man. You've been in denial for five years. You *hate* him. You're about to make me sick with all this pious 'I forgive this person' stuff...you *hate* him. Now that you've gotten in touch with the fact that you hate him, maybe we can get some healing going here."

And I did—I mean I hated this guy. I didn't know it until I found it out. I had a fiery chunk of hate down inside of me. And I had to face that hate before I could move toward forgiveness.

You may have the same feeling toward someone, too. Step Eight brings us the opportunity to rid ourselves of that hate through forgiveness. Remember "to err is human, to forgive is divine." But in our human condition, we're powerless to forgive anyone. Therefore, we have to have the Spirit of God in us to empower us to forgive.

Bottom line

There are other people that we have harmed through our own self-centeredness—self-centered fear, self-pity, self-service, self-will, self-propulsion, ambition.

We've made decisions based on self that have placed us in a position to be harmed by others.

We've made decisions based on self that just flat out caused us to harm or take advantage of others.

Those that we've harmed need to go on the list in Step Eight, and we need to be willing to make the amends.

Self-examination - amends list

Here are areas to look at as you continue to complete your amends list.

Have you caused somebody monetary loss? Have you stolen their money, or cheated them out of their money, or caused them to lose money somehow? Maybe you've broken a contract or damaged their property.

Have you harmed someone's reputation? Have you assassinated their character, or slandered their name, or spread gossip?

Have you harmed somebody mentally or emotionally? Have you reacted to them in anger, or put them down, or manipulated their feelings? Have you caused verbal abuse with your words and the attitudes behind them? Have you been neglectful of others? Selfishly preoccupied? Broken your promises?

Have you caused moral harm? Have you gotten others involved in your harmful behavior? Have you caused others to go against their conscience? Have you done things to others (including your employer, insurance company, etc.) that were unethical or unfair? Have you set a bad example for your children?

Have you physically harmed somebody?

Have you spiritually harmed others or spoken curses over them? Have you been manipulative in controlling their religious doctrines?

Any control or manipulation or self-centered activity with other human beings constitutes harm. One of the ways that you harm them is in using your controlling ways to manipulate them into your will for their lives because of self-will or your own self-centered desires.

As you look over your amends list, check these things: Did you *harm* this person? If so, what did you do to harm this person? What kind of harm did you cause this person? How can you best make amends for that harm?

——— STEP EIGHT - ACTION ———

In Step Four we made our moral inventory and made a list of resentments, amends, and defects. By now we've probably added to those lists. In Step Seven, we humbly asked God to remove the shortcomings or defects. Now it's time to move toward making the amends. We don't make those amends just yet, but in this step we complete our list of amends and "become willing to the list"—willing to go face to face, or pick up the phone, or write a letter asking for forgiveness.

Take a moment before going on to meditate upon the step.

Made a list of all persons we had harmed and became willing to make amends to them all.

Pride and fear are the two main things that stand in the way of our courageously making amends to someone we have injured. Becoming "willing to the list" is our way of pulling down that stronghold of pride or fear, giving us the confidence to take Step Nine where we actually make the amends. So, the whole purpose of this step is to finish the list and become "willing to the list."

A. *Taking Action*

Here are areas to look at as you continue to complete your amends list:

1. To whom have you caused monetary loss? From whom have you stolen money? Whom have you cheated out of money? Whom have you caused to lose money somehow? With whom have you broken a contract? Whose property have you damaged?

2. Whose reputation have you harmed? Whose character have you assassinated? Whose name have you slandered? About whom have you spread gossip?

3. Whom have you harmed mentally or emotionally? To whom have you reacted in anger? Whom have you put down? Whose feelings have you manipulated? To whom have you caused verbal abuse with your words and the attitudes behind them?

4. Of whom have you been neglectful? Who has suffered from your selfish preoccupations?

5. To whom have you broken your promises?

6. To whom have you caused moral harm? Whom have you involved in your harmful behavior? Whom have you caused to go against his/her conscience?

7. To whom have you done things (including your employer, insurance company, etc.) that were unethical or unfair?

8. Do you owe your children an amend for setting a bad example?

9. Whom have you physically harmed?

10. Whom have you spiritually harmed and brought curses upon? With whom have you been manipulative in controlling religious doctrines?

11. As you look over your amends list, check these things:
Did you *harm* this person?
If so, what did you do to harm this person?
What kind of harm did you cause this person?
How can you best make amends for that harm?

12. Go back over your list of amends. Is your list accurate and complete?

13. Are those on your list the names of people you have harmed and not just people whom you want to try to get to like you?

14. Are you truly willing to make amends to everyone on your list—not only to say I'm sorry, but to do whatever the other person says it takes to make restitution?

15. If there are amends on your list that you are not willing to make, what are they?

16. Why are you not willing to make those amends?

17. How is pride blocking you from making amends?

18. What resentments do you still have that are blocking you from making an amend?

19. What fears do you have that are blocking you from making amends?

20. What will it take for you to become willing to make amends to certain ones on your list?

21. Are you now willing to take the initiative to make these amends?

22. Are you willing to let God bring about the opportunities for making amends in circumstances where you do not know how to get in touch with certain ones on your list or how to go about making particular amends?

B. *In your journal:*
   1. What changes have you experienced today in your thoughts, feelings, or behaviors as the result of taking this step?
   2. In what ways have you discovered God or sensed His presence in your life?
   3. What victories have you had?
   4. What defeats have you had?

STEP NINE

Made direct amends to such people wherever possible except when to do so would injure them or others.

There are two parts to Step Nine: (1) "made direct amends wherever possible" and (2) "except when to do so would injure them or others."

Made direct amends wherever possible

When we did our fourth and fifth steps, we came up with a list of our amends, our defects, and our resentments. We bring the amends list forward to Steps Eight and Nine. In Step Eight we became "willing to the list." That's all we had to do.

As we become willing, a rather miraculous thing happens. A transformation occurs inside of us concerning our approaching these individuals, and sometimes individuals whom you thought were nowhere to be found reappear in your life.

A personal story

After some time of working this process in my life, I had done another fourth and fifth step. I had brought my list to the eighth step and was ready to make amends in the ninth step.

There was a certain individual that I had harmed rather severely, both financially and emotionally, and I had also assassinated his character somewhat. I had to make amends to this fellow. I had known the fellow both drinking and sober, but I hadn't seen the fellow in about ten years. He lived in Tucson, Arizona, and I lived in Missouri. This was not an economically fruitful time in my life, and there was no way for me to get to Tucson even if I could find this guy.

I was working in the music business with a full-blooded American Indian who had an album out. I did all the booking for him. One day my phone rang and it was the Papago Indians on the reservation just outside of Tucson, Arizona. This was right when I had this guy from Tucson on my amends list, and I had just gotten to Step Nine.

They wanted to hire this musician. I said, "Okay," and made the arrangements.

When I told the fellow about it, he said, "O'Neil, I'm not going unless you go. You've got to call them back and tell them, 'It's no deal unless you bring O'Neil with me.' I'm not going out there by myself."

So, I called them back and said, "Look, I know you don't have that much money, but if this guy is going to come, then I'll have to come as his manager."

And they said, "Okay. That's no problem. How much will that be?"

So, all of a sudden, within forty-eight hours of becoming willing to make amends, I had a round-trip plane ticket, expenses, and a place to stay in Tucson, Arizona.

I called information, got the phone number, and when I got my friend on the phone, he said that he and another fellow that I owed amends to would pick me up at the airport.

So, within two weeks of being willing to make amends to this person whom I hadn't seen in ten years, with no idea of how I would find him or get there if I could find him, I was sitting in his car at the airport. We were able to spend some time together and I was able to make some life-long amends. I had spent many years with these two gentlemen—it wasn't just a one-time thing. We had been dear friends for a long time, and my drinking and drug use had ruined all that. So, it was real special and very interesting. Of course, when God starts working, it's always *real* interesting.

When you become willing in Step Eight—watch out. Watch out for those names on that list. God's likely to put them in front of you in the line at the grocery store.

Wherever possible

We try through whatever means possible to contact the people that are on our list that we owe amends to. Telephone them. Write them a letter. Call them and make an appointment to see them face-to-face. Hopefully, we can see them face-to-face—that's the best.

Amends

There are two parts to making amends—the apology and the restitution.

Apology

The first part of it is saying "I'm sorry." We apologize for whatever it is. We might say, "When this was going on I was emotionally disturbed," or "I was on drugs," or "I was out of my mind," or whatever... "and I'm sorry. Will you forgive me?"

During that particular time, we focus on ourselves. We're willing to admit our faults. Remember that these are *our* amends, not the other person's. We are trying to get at peace with this other person.

It's not our purpose to get that person to acknowledge the fact that he was also a jerk during the time that this was going on. So, we stay away from details and conversations like, "Well, you know, I'm sorry, but if you hadn't started it, then I wouldn't have ever been the way I was," or "You always acted like you were better than I was, and I couldn't stand that, so I had to get back at you." No, that's not an amend. We stay completely away from that.

We own our inventory and our part of the action, and we deliver that information, and we make the amends. If they wish to say, "Well, you know, I had some part in that, too...," we just shake our head, or nod, or say, "Well, if you'd like to say that, that's fine." But don't run with that. In other words, if they say, "Well, you know, I wasn't such a great guy," don't get started with, "Now that you mention it..."

Restitution

The second part of making amends is the restitution. We should follow up our apology with a statement such as, "What can I do to make this right?"

The easiest example of restitution, or making things right, is monetary amends—when you go to someone that you owe money to.

You might say to the fellow, "I'm really sorry that I beat you out of that thousand dollars and now I'm in this program and I'm changing my life. I'm going to be a good guy, and I'm not going to beat people out of their money any more. And I just need you to forgive me."

And he says, "Well, I forgive you, but where's my thousand dollars?"

Well, we don't get off with, "Oh, well, man, I don't have the thousand dollars. I was just kinda hoping that...uh...you know, with me being humble and coming over and telling you this, that you'd just forget about it." Well, no.

We say, "What can I do to make this right?"

The person says, "Well, you can pay me my thousand dollars."

We say, "I would like to do that, but I don't have a thousand dollars."

So, he says, "Well, what do you have?"

We check our pocket and say, "I have five dollars."

And the person says, "I'll take it." Then we may set up some payments.

When I began my walk in the Twelve Steps, I owed an accountant a rather large amount of money from some previous business deals. I had told him, "Just do the work and I'll pay you."

When I came to my eighth and ninth step, I owed this man amends and I owed him money. I hadn't paid him and I hadn't attempted to pay him and I had avoided him. So I saw him and I told him that I was sorry and that I was an alcoholic. He said, "Well, I'm glad you found that out, we all already knew it anyway."

So I said, "I want to make this right, and all I can do right now is send you five dollars a month."

And he said, "I'll take it."

That was in 1973, and in 1991 I finally paid it off. I doubled up on the payments a couple of times, even sent him twenty dollars once. In early 1991 I had a balance finally of twenty dollars. I wrote him a check for a whole twenty dollars, and I wrote him a note and sent it to him and paid it off. That's eighteen years at five bucks a month. Won't buy you a house, but it will pay off somebody that you owe money to.

He used to send me notes about every third month. "Mike, thanks for the regular payments."

So, don't think that you have to stomp into the banker with your chest puffed out and that thousand dollars wadded up in your hands, ready to slam it down on his desk and say, "Here's your money!" Just go in there and say, "Here's what I can do." And *do* it. And you'll be amazed at what the response is from people—*if you do it*.

So, what comes after the apology is the restitution. The restitution is equally important, if not more important, than the apology. Together they constitute the amends.

In some cases we have to make restitution before we can get face to face to make the apology, such as in the case of back child support. The ex-husband resides out-of-state, and the wife is putting down charges to have the guy arrested. She's not interested in hearing his little voice on the other end of the phone or seeing his little face. She wants to see a check. If she does see his face in town, she'll have him arrested. So, the check, the restitution, or the beginning of the restitution is sometimes the way to work toward the opportunity to make the apology.

Forgive yourself

There's another thing about the amends that's important to mention. We have to make amends to one more person—*ourselves*. We need to forgive ourselves—we really do.

This is the final piece in self-forgiveness and in making peace with ourselves, so that we can be that new creature in Christ that we've been trying to be and haven't been able to be. Forgive yourself, so that you can give yourself permission to be who God wants you to be.

When I do this, I get down on my knees and go through the things that I've done to myself. They're there in my fourth step, but I usually don't have to look at my fourth step, because they're also right there in my head—I know what they are. I list the self-destructive things that I've continued to do and make amends to myself. I tell myself, "I haven't been very good to you. I've treated you pretty rotten. I'd like to ask your forgiveness."

If you'd like to separate it out more, go back to the shame-based stuff with the shame corral that generates a false self. Separate this false, phoney self over here from the real you, and recognize that he's harmed you. He needs to make amends to you, and then he needs to just die and go away.

Except when to do so would injure them or others

Now, the other aspect of making the amends that I want to talk about is "except when to do so would injure them or others."

There's two others. There's "them" and "others." And *we* are one of the others. We don't make amends when it's going to harm us.

Also, we don't rush into amends when someone is still stinging from the last hit. Maybe we don't want them to be mad at us anymore, so we want to hurry up and get this peace made and get them to be okay—but that's not the time to make the amends. Sometimes we need to let the dust settle.

Others

The main examples of harm to others is usually in the area of family or marriage, and the best example is infidelity.

You don't go to the wife or the husband and say, "Honey, I'm working my eighth and ninth step here, and I've been a little bit untrue a couple of times...well, more than a couple...it's more like thirty or forty. And I just wanted to make amends to you for that, and, of course, I have all their names here—I'd like to list them for you. There was Sally, and Janie, and then you remember your sister? Well, it was...you know, it was just one night..."

We don't do that. We just don't do that. That causes harm to *them and others*—you being one of the others. It's extremely destructive.

The rule of thumb is this: *we can't get well at the expense of another person.* Okay? Let me emphasize that: you can't get deliverance or get well at the expense of another person.

This is *our* inventory and *our* amends. It's not theirs.

Freedom from resentments

Freedom from resentments is one of the major things that comes out of Step Nine. Resentments are the number one cause of our continuing in self-destructive behavior and continuing to involve ourselves in self-pity. If we can hang on to hate and resentment for other people, then we can justify our behavior and our actions and then we can feel sorry for ourselves. And if we work it just right, we can get others to feel sorry for ourselves with us.

So when we come down to Steps Eight and Nine, we really shoot a torpedo at the resentments. This is designed to put those away once and for all.

The people that are on our amends list are generally on our resentment list, too. If so, that means that we owe amends to the people on the resentment list. We need to make some amends for resenting them.

Now, that doesn't mean we go harm them by saying, "You know, I've always hated your guts. First time I ever saw you, you just made me mad, and I've hated you ever since. I think you're a jerk and I resent you a lot... See you." That's not what we do.

We go in and make an amends for our feelings of aggression and hate and anger and resentment for these people. Big difference.

Sometimes it's really hard to get far enough past the resentment to be able to make the amend in a right attitude. When this happens, it helps to write a hate letter.

For example, there's a father or mother or someone who may still be alive that you really have some severe hate for or anger toward. You write anger letters or hate letters to those people, *letters that you won't ever send.* But you may read them to your Twelve Step group if you have one, or read them to your sponsor, or you may go through some sort of exercise of reading them out loud to God, to try to dispel some of that anger.

Before we can get rid of the problem, we have to own the problem. That's the main purpose for writing the letter. So, we write the letter, and we read the letter.

Oftentimes when we have a deep hate, resentment, or anger toward someone, we try to forgive him and try to forgive him and try to forgive him—and we just can't. We just can't. We once again find that we are powerless to do that. So we have to go back in there, taking Jesus with us through this process, and embrace that hate. The goal is not to hate him, but we do have to own it—own that inventory, and then begin to work through it and face it.

I find that if you live in that hate for a while, if you write those letters and you live with that for a while, face to face, day to day, you get a little sick of it. In fact you get real sick of it.

One of the things that I do with clients in this area is have them write that hate letter and then bring it to me. Then I have them rewrite it, so that it's *really* a hate letter. Then I have them read it everyday. On their knees. And then pray.

I could show you one I wrote...if I still had it. I burned it. I don't have to read it any more.

God can only meet you where you are. He can't meet you where you're going to be or where you used to be or where you wish you were.

Procrastination

There is a tendency to procrastinate on Step Nine. All of the procrastination is rooted in fear. We have to get past the fear, roll up our shirtsleeves, and go in there and make the amends.

Some of the things we procrastinate with are, "Well, let's just let bygones be bygones."

Or "They hurt me a little bit; I hurt them a little bit—mmmm, I think it's even. We'll just let it go."

Or "God'll take care of it. I prayed about that last year and I let it go and I'm sure it's okay now."

Or, we avoid that person—we find an excuse to drive around the block if we see them.

Another procrastination is twisting or rationalizing this phrase, "when to make an amend would harm them or others." We'll twist that around in our brains until we're convinced that to make an amend to this person would harm them or harm ourselves when that's not the truth.

Take action

We've written our list, we've looked at it, we've thought about it, we've read this chapter—and that's all a part of it—but it doesn't mean anything until you put it all into action. This spiritual life that we're entering into isn't just theory. What makes the difference, what gives you some peace and deliverance, is the action. So, get on the phone and call that person, write that person a letter, go face to face, make the appointment, make the amends. Get through it and get past it.

If you owe an amend to someone who has died, write him a letter.

This was the case for me with my father. I had made some amends to him, but I hadn't made some other amends to him that I needed to make. So, I wrote him a letter and, in a prayerful fashion on my knees, I read him that letter out loud. And I'm at peace with all that now. It sounds like maybe it wouldn't work, but it does—if God's in it.

A right attitude

So, when we make amends, we go to the individuals with a forgiving attitude. We don't mumble and beat around the bush. We're calm and honest and to the point. We're considerate and go to them in humility.

Another story

After taking the fourth through ninth steps again, I had to make amends to someone for the harm that I did him. I went to him and made an amend while he was still stinging from the harm. He told me, "Well, O'Neil, you know, you were a jerk. I never knew you when you were drinking; I didn't meet you 'til you sobered up. But you were a jerk sober. As far as I'm concerned, you're still a jerk."

I said, "Thank you very much. I appreciate that. I just thought I'd make my amends." And I left.

Then I ran into the fellow that sponsored me. He had just, by coincidence, run into the man the day before. He said to me, "My God, man, what did you do to so-and-so?"

I said, "Well…I…nothing."

"You're supposed to go make amends to that guy!" he said.

I said, "Well, I did. I made amends. I went in there and told him the deal, and, you know, I made amends."

"Didn't work!"

"Well, that's his problem," I said. "I did my part—it's his problem."

"No, it's *your* problem. You gotta go back."

"Oh, no, man. Don't make me go back in there."

But I had to go back. Call him back up. Go back. Make amends. Sit down with him. And *really* get humble, and *really* apologize to this guy. And get real with him. When I did that, things turned out fine. That was many years ago. That man and I are very close friends now.

But had I not gone back, done what I was told, and made a genuine amends with the humility and sincerity that God would want, it still wouldn't be right. You see, the first time I went in there, I was about as angry at him as he was at me. I went in with that, "Well, I'm sorry!"—like when you get those two kids together and say, "Now, you tell her you're sorry," and, "You tell him you're sorry." I went in there like that, and that wasn't going to get it. He wasn't buying it. But when I went back with a different attitude, a different heart, and sincerity about what I had to say, then it worked.

Check yourself out

So, if you make your amend and it doesn't work, if somebody doesn't forgive, you'll want to check and see if you did it right—see if you made a genuine amend. Sometimes we're not sure—I didn't know I hadn't done it right.

What you'll need to do is go back and retake Steps Four and Five on that situation. Check your attitude. Did I go in there still resenting this guy? Did I blame him? Even if my words were okay, was I being self-righteous? Did I really address the amends? What really happened?

Examine those things *and* talk to your sponsor about it. Go to another individual, just like you should be doing through this whole process, to keep yourself honest with yourself.

This process is not designed for you to work by yourself. It's designed for you to have another person to mirror your work. Go to your sponsor or the person that you trust that's working the program with you and say, "Here's what I did, here's what I think, here's what happened, here's the results. What does that feel like and sound like to you?"

Get the feedback. "Here's what I wrote in my fourth step about it."

If that person says, "Well, if what you're saying is the truth, and you did have that kind of heart and that kind of spirit, then you did make an amend, and you can just go on." (You don't need to get codependent where you're running around just trying to get people to like you.)

This step is designed to work. These steps, Eight and Nine, are designed to fix it. They really are. This is not just an exercise because you don't have anything to do on Saturday afternoon. It's designed to fix the problem.

Now sometimes, if the other person is unable to accept your apology or amends, but you made it in the right spirit, and you're going to make the restitution necessary, then it *is* their problem, and it's for them to work out with God. But most of the time, it will work. It will miraculously transform the situation that you're in. For both parties.

Peace

So, we make our direct amends where possible. We write, call, go face-to-face, and when we get to the end of our list, or even halfway down our list, we begin to start feeling a tremendous release from this bondage of resentment and hate that's been on us all of our lives.

Some of you have been holding things against people in your family of origin, either alive or dead, for your whole life. They're not going to change, but you can change. If you can get through Steps Eight and Nine, you'll get tremendous relief from that bondage.

I call Steps Four through Nine "death valley." This is the last step in "death valley." When we've taken this step, we should be feeling peace with God, peace with ourselves, and peace with others, which pretty much covers the spectrum of who we can be at war with.

We're at peace, maybe for the first time in our whole lives. A peace that passes all understanding that Jesus talked about.

And we should begin to feel good about ourselves. We should stop, at this point, beating ourselves up so much and ruminating in our minds. We should start feeling some self-worth and some self-esteem.

Promises

This is what the book *Alcoholics Anonymous* says about Step Nine:
> If we are painstaking about this phase of our development, we will be amazed before we are half way through.
> We are going to know a new freedom and a new happiness.
> We will not regret the past nor wish to shut the door on it.
> We will comprehend the word serenity and we will know peace.

No matter how far down the scale we have gone, we will see how our experience can benefit others.

That feeling of uselessness and self-pity will disappear.

We will lose interest in selfish things and gain interest in our fellows.

Self-seeking will slip away.

Our whole attitude and outlook upon life will change.

Fear of people and of economic insecurity will leave us.

We will intuitively know how to handle situations which used to baffle us.

We will suddenly realize that God is doing for us what we could not do for ourselves.[1]

---

[1]*Alcoholics Anonymous*, p. 83-84.

STEP NINE - ACTION

We need to seek forgiveness in three different directions. First, we need to receive God's forgiveness as we deal with our own defects. Secondly, we need to forgive others, whereby we deal with our own resentments. Thirdly, we seek to be forgiven by those we've harmed as we make our amends.

Having done these things, we have successfully begun to make peace with God, ourselves, and others. Until all three areas of forgiveness have been successfully dealt with, there will remain remnants of war in our souls.

Meditate on this step before going on:

Make direct amends to such people wherever possible, except when to do so would injure them or others.

The purpose of this step is to make peace with those others whom you have harmed by going to them in one way or another, asking their forgiveness, making restitution if possible, and thereby making your amends.

A. *Taking Action*

Good timing is crucial in taking this step. Having resolved to make direct amends wherever possible, pray to God to give you that perfect sense of timing and then promptly go to those persons, telephone them, or write them a letter.

There is a caution written into this step which says, "except when to do so would injure them or others." You need to be totally honest with yourself and not use that statement as a cop-out for not making an amends to someone when you really need to.

Remember that it's your job to get at peace with others, not to manipulate others into being at peace with you.

Check yourself out:

1. How are you using the caution in this step as a cop-out for not making amends to somebody that you may owe amends to?

2. Are you prepared to do whatever it takes in Step Nine to make it right?

3. Have you planned the ways you're going to make amends to the people on your list, either by telephone, writing them a letter, or seeing them in person?

4. What are some of the things that you may have to be willing to do to make things right between you and another person?

Having made amends, or some amends, or attempted to do so:
5. What was the outcome of those amends you have made or attempted to make?

6. Have you found someone who was unwilling to forgive you?   If so, what have you done about that, if anything?

The following questions are based on the Step Nine promises. After you have made some amends, check yourself out:
7. In what ways do you now know a new freedom and happiness that you did not have before?

8. How do you now feel about your past and how you wanted to shut the door on it?

9. Are you more serene and do you know peace?

10. How do you see your experience as benefiting others?

11. Do you feel more useful?

12. Has self-pity disappeared?

13. How are you more aware of others and their needs?

14. How are you less self-seeking?

15. How has your overall outlook on life changed?

16. Do you have less fear of other people?

17. Are you more secure regarding your economic situation?

18. Do you now intuitively know how to handle situations that used to baffle you?

19. What is God doing for you now what you could not do for yourself?

B. *In your journal:*
1. What changes have you experienced today in your thoughts, feelings, or behaviors as the result of taking this step?
2. In what ways have you discovered God or sensed His presence in your life?
3. What victories have you had?
4. What defeats have you had?

**Continued to take personal inventory
and when we were wrong promptly admitted it.**

In Steps One through Nine we've put our house in order, or tried to. Hopefully, we've changed or interrupted destructive behaviors that have been causing us something less than success in some, or maybe all, areas of our lives.

We can wipe our brow and say, "Boy, I'm glad that's done, and I won't ever have to do that again." Well, you just won't have to do the same things with the same people that you did it with the first time. You see, Step Ten puts us back into the system—it throws us back into Steps Four through Nine, and also thrusts us forward to Step Twelve. It puts us into the process of **maintenance and growth.**

The book *Alcoholics Anonymous* says,

> This thought brings us to Step Ten, which suggests we continue to take personal inventory and continue to set right any new mistakes as we go along. We vigorously commenced this way of living as we cleaned up the past. We have entered the world of the Spirit. Our next function is to grow in understanding and effectiveness. This is not an overnight matter. It should continue for our lifetime. Continue to watch for selfishness, dishonesty, resentment, and fear. When these crop up, we ask God at once to remove them. We discuss them with someone immediately and make amends quickly if we have harmed anyone. Then we resolutely turn our thoughts to someone we can help. Love and tolerance of others is our code.[1]

Those are our instructions:
It says, "We have entered the world of the Spirit." So, now we're living

---

[1]*Alcoholics Anonymous*, p. 84.

a spiritual life.

Then it says that our recovery is "not an overnight matter," it's a lifetime process.

It says that we "continue to take personal inventory...watch for selfishness, dishonesty, resentment, and fear."

When we discover these things, we identify them, then we talk to another person about them as soon as possible.

We ask God to remove these defects as soon as we discover them.

If we've wronged anybody, we ask them to forgive us.

After we do that, we turn our thoughts to someone else.

Can you see what steps we're going back to?

We continue to look for defects, like resentment—that's Step Four.

We're going to tell somebody—that's Step Five.

We're going to ask God to remove the defects—Steps Six and Seven.

We make amends to somebody that we've harmed—Eight and Nine.

And then we jump to Step Twelve—we're going to turn our thoughts to someone else. "Love and tolerance is our code."

So Step Ten throws us back into Steps Four through Nine plus Step Twelve. That's the particular, mapped-out plan of Step Ten, which is kind of ingenious, I think.

In the overview we said that Steps Ten and Eleven are the maintenance or growth steps out of the Twelve Steps. You can see how Step Ten ties into maintenance. Now, one of the old sayings is that "we take the Steps, so that we can learn how to take the Steps, so that we can take the Steps." So, as we come into Step Ten, that adage begins to come true.

Continued to take personal inventory

There are three kinds of inventories: an ongoing inventory, a daily inventory, and a periodic inventory.

Ongoing inventory

The ongoing inventory is what we do throughout the day.

As we're moving through the day, Barney comes along and says something to us, and it makes us mad. It makes us feel angry...hurt... inferior, and so we want to hurt or get back at Barney.

We try to identify those feelings (Step Four); and we also try to get past the emotion and withhold our explosive reaction.

Then if we can, we talk to another person (Step Five), and if we can't talk to another person right then, we go immediately to Steps Six and Seven and ask God to remove this—"I've got terrific anger. Explosive rage is welling up inside of me. Please, God, remove that." Then maybe later we can find someone to talk to about it, our sponsor preferably, or someone in the Twelve Step program who understands what we are doing.

If we did explode and go off on Barney—if we told him what for and harmed him, then we need to go on to Steps Eight and Nine as fast as we can. We need to promptly admit we were wrong. And we don't just admit it to God, or to the air. We go in there and say, "Look, man, what you said made me feel rejected and insecure and hurt, and then I got angry. Instead of talking it out with you, I lost my temper. I was wrong for doing that, and I'm sorry." We do that instead of tucking that little piece away in our little box, putting it down there and thinking, "That's just one more for Barney. He just about filled his quota."

If we stuff these feelings, an interesting phenomenon occurs when Barney's quota begins to fill up—we become a victim of what's called "displaced anger." We go home at night and our youngest child comes running up to us and says, "Daddy, daddy, I've been asking you for three days to fix my bicycle and you haven't fixed my bicycle, and I really want you to fix it. Would you go out there and fix it?"

And we promptly pick that child up, shake him profusely, and then go into an over-reactive rage at this child saying, "Shut up and get out of my face!" when all the while it's Barney we're angry at, not the child.

Daily inventory

Our second kind of inventory is a daily inventory.

At the end of the day, we look over the past activities and events of the day, reviewing where we might have harmed someone, or where we acted out in fear, anger, resentment, self-pity, selfishness, or self-centeredness. If we've harmed anyone, we can make amends to that person as soon as possible.

We also look at the things that we may have done right throughout the day. Believe it or not, we actually do some things right. We list those, and we say, "That wasn't bad. You know, I had victory over that right there. That was good. I achieved that goal. I haven't been able to do that before. I did withhold my explosive anger with God's help." So, we list our victories, too.

We spend about ten or fifteen minutes at the end of the day to do that.

Periodic inventory

The periodic inventory is taken once or twice a year.

We may go on a retreat to do this. We may set aside a weekend for it. Or we may sit down and do as much as we can, as we're able. We do a formal inventory of the fourth step, starting from the last time that we took an inventory.

In one of my formal inventories I discovered an area in my life that I had never inventoried. Since I had never covered that particular part of my past life, I chose to reach back and pull that forward.

So, though it's not always the case, sometimes when we take a periodic inventory to bring ourselves forward from the last inventory, it might trigger something that we want to look at from the past. Even though we've already inventoried those years, we go ahead and do that.

So we write a periodic inventory, and we take a formal fifth step, and go though Six, Seven, Eight, and Nine with our list. We keep that house cleaned out. Remember, in Steps One through Nine we get our house in order, and we've hopefully interrupted destructive behaviors. We want to keep that house in order as much as possible.

When we were wrong, promptly admitted it

When it comes to "promptly admitted we were wrong," I came to a place in my recovery where I had to decide whether I was going to be right or be happy. Am I going to be right? "I'm *so* right! And I don't care what anyone thinks, and I don't care what they say, I'm right! I'm miserable, and I want to methodically character-assassinate this guy, but I'm *right!*"

Sometimes being right can nearly kill you. I'd rather be free than right. One of the defects we look for in Step Four is self-righteousness.

Another is dishonesty. And who are we dishonest with? Ourselves. That's who we're mostly dishonest with through our rationalization and self-pity. Remember, I can take a situation, including being right, and rationalize it into self-pity. I can justify every behavior. It doesn't matter what it is. I can justify all my resentments, all my anger, all my hate, all my addictions, all my compulsive, obsessive workaholism—anything. And once I rationalize myself into feeling sorry for myself, I'm content in my misery. Then, like I've said before, if I can find another melonhead like myself to get in there and feel sorry for me with me, then I'm on a roll.

There's an old saying, "Poor me. Poor me. Pour me another drink."

Goals

Now, the inventories that we take, both in Step Four and then in Ten, help us discover who we are, what we are, and where we're going.

So, one of the things that I've started doing in my ongoing tenth step, is to set some goals. Goal-setting has been one of the most positive tools that I've discovered in getting my life in order and seeing it return to a manageable form.

However, there is more to goal-setting than just writing a big wish list on a piece of paper.

I learned that goal-setting needs to be a very focused and concrete activity. I start with a piece of paper and divide it into columns. Each column represents a time-frame for a particular goal—for instance a one-year goal, a six-month goal, a one-month goal, and a one-week goal. I decide where I want to be or what I want to have accomplished in one year. Then I decide where I want to be or what I want to have done in six months to help me get to the one-year goal. Next I decide what I want to do in one month that will get me to my six-month goal. And finally, I decide what I need to do in one week to reach the one-month goal. All of that should fit into how I'm going to get where I want to be in one year.

For a simple example of this, let's use a financial goal. Let's say in one year I want to have twelve hundred dollars in a savings account. So, in six months, I want to have at least six hundred dollars in a savings account. In one month I want to have one hundred dollars in a savings account. And in one week, I want to have at least twenty-five dollars in a savings account. That tells me that every week, I want to put at least twenty-five dollars in my savings account.

$$\$1,200 \text{ in one year} = \$600 \text{ in six months}$$
$$\$600 \text{ in six months} = \$100 \text{ per month}$$
$$\$100 \text{ per month} = \$25 \text{ per week}$$

The more concrete you can make the action aspects of your written goal-setting, the more realistic your goals will be and the simpler they'll be.

For example: "I want to clean out my garage—it's been a mess for five years." What we generally do is decide to go out there on Saturday afternoon and completely tear everything out of our garage, and clean the whole thing out and make it perfect. But then we procrastinate and we don't do it. So, if it's a job like that, then we can decide, "In one month I want to have my garage straightened out, and this week I will begin in the southwest corner, and on Saturday I will work for two hours throwing things away in the southwest corner." (You may have to start with the front door, I don't know, depending on how bad the garage is.) But decide on very concrete, specific actions.

Break your objectives down into daily goals. I find, for myself, that if I look at my general goal sheet at the end of the day and write down what I need to do tomorrow, that I end up getting those daily goals done in maybe the first couple of hours of the next day. But if I wait to do it the next day, I spend the first hour or so figuring out what I'm going to do that day. If you can get your daily goals out of the way in the first couple of hours of your day, then you have a free rein for what's going to go on in the afternoon. And that includes things on your job.

In a specific life area, I usually ask myself these four questions:
1. Where am I in this life area right now?
2. Where do I want to be?
3. When do I want to be there?
4. How am I going to get there?

Here are some life areas for you to look at. You can ask the four questions about them and write goals around them, giving yourself some sort of time frame to reach the goals.

Life area	Where am I?	Where do I want to be?	When do I want to be there?	How am I going to get there?
Spiritual				

Sobriety (but don't think of that as a drunk trying to be sober, but as being whole-minded—wholeness of mind and spirit. Think about what sobriety means in your particular situation. What is it you're trying to gain victory over—workaholism? people addictions? relationships?)

| Family | | | | |

Life area	Where am I?	Where do I I want to be?	When do I want to be there?	How am I going to get there?
Relationships				
Social				
Physical				
Emotional				
Educational				
Financial				
Career				

(This is a generic list that I use in making goals for myself. You might have an area you'd like to add for yourself.)

If you're looking at finances, ask yourself, "Where am I in my finances? Where do I want to be in my finances? When do I want to be there? And how am I going to get there?" Then come up with a plan to implement that goal on a daily, weekly, and monthly basis, with a check-point down the road.

When I first started saving, I started saving with five dollars a week. I had to break the mind-set that says, "If I can't put a hundred dollars in, what's the sense in putting only five dollars in the savings account?" But after you put five dollars a week in the savings account, pretty soon it's twenty, and then it's fifty, and, before you know it, you've got something!

When I had my first thousand dollars in a savings account, I couldn't believe it. I had graduated to where I put more than five dollars a week in there, but I started with five dollars. It was unbelievable. And it was a thousand dollars that was just there. It didn't have to go on the rent, and it didn't have to go on the car payment—somebody's name wasn't on that thousand dollars. It was a great feeling of accomplishment.

So goal-setting is a positive thing to put into your maintenance package for growth and achievement in your recovery, so you won't just beat yourself up for the mistakes that you're making all the time. One time after another, "Well, I tried to do this and I failed again. I failed again." After the ninth step, we leave crisis-to-crisis living and we move into prevention and growth living; and when a crisis does occur, we're more prepared to do something about it.

You're worth it

We are not very self-disciplined. We codependents, ego-maniacs with inferiority complexes, obsessive-compulsive personalities, people with disorders, alcoholics, chemical-dependent, people-dependent maniacs—we have a lot of trouble with self-discipline. (The possible exception is the person whose addiction is discipline.)

But in order to pay attention to these kinds of things and put discipline in our lives, we've got to think we're worthy of attaining these accomplishments. You know, I have an overwhelming tendency to help someone else achieve his goals before I begin to pay any attention to mine.

So, getting that self-discipline in there is directly tied to my thinking I'm *worth* having some self-discipline, or that I'm worth having twelve hundred dollars in my savings account instead of giving it away to somebody I think needs it more than I do.

Self-discipline—it's very difficult for us, but realistic goal-setting is a tool to help us get going on it.

Some of you might worry about setting goals for self instead of for God. But as we drop our baggage in Steps Four through Nine, we find out that what we want is what God wants. I mean, it really is. Hopefully, by Step Ten, we've gotten away from self—we've gotten somewhat out of self-centeredness, self-serving, self-pity, and self-propulsion. After all, what we've been working on up to this point is getting God's will for us into our lives.

Our lives had become unmanageable in certain areas when we began this process. But by the time we get to Step Ten, hopefully, our thinking has cleared up and we have become more God-centered than self-centered.

Promises

Let me give you a few of my own promises for Step Ten.

The first one: As our reactions to people change, *troubled relationships will begin to disappear.* I want you to think about how important that is. We can't get away from relationships.

If I go and live on a mountain in Colorado and the only person that I see is me and somebody down in the little town where I get my supplies once a week—then I have very few problems. My problems are the squirrels that got in my cookies. But when I come down from the mountain and I get in a room full of people, and I have to begin to have *relationships* with them, all kinds of problems start coming up.

I don't know if that's bad or good, that's just the way it is. And what did God say? Was it "Love the Lord thy God with your whole heart and your whole soul and your whole mind, and go live on a mountain in Colorado?" No, that isn't what He said.

Jesus said, "You shall love the Lord thy God with all your heart, and with all your soul, and with all your mind, and with all your strength...and you shall love your neighbor as yourself."[2]

Well, now I've got problems. That means I've got to love you. I don't have to like you, but I've got to love you, and I've got to be in a relationship with you. But I have trouble with relationships with other human beings. When I have to have a relationship with other human beings, all of the things that we talked about in that inventory begin to reoccur and stick their little heads up and start running my life. So, relationships are where most of my problems occur. And so, having this promise in my life is very important.

---

[2]Mark 12:30-31

Another promise is that *we begin to drop the false front,* or that false self that we've talked about that's been created from our shame-based person. This false person goes out and has these relationships with everybody while we sit back and watch. We judge it, and we go, "Look what he's doing now. Oh, let's see what that one's doing. Here, we need to throw one of these in on 'em." We sit back and watch that false self having that relationship with another false person.

So, as we come to Step Ten, we begin to drop that false self. We begin to become real and be who we really are in Christ, and we take our real self into relationships with others.

Another promise is *freedom from guilt.* Wouldn't that be nice?—since toxic guilt has plagued most of us all of our lives.

Another one—we've become *able to help others.* We can do that now because of our own recovery. We're able to be real because we are admitting our wrongs and our faults and taking that pressure off of ourselves to be perfect. We can be a human being instead of a human doing. Though we strive for perfection, we're settling for progress.

Finally

In Step Ten we continue to clear the baggage that blocks us off from the sunlight of God's Spirit. Now that we have begun to experience some of the wholeness He has prepared for us through His Son, Jesus Christ, we will want to grow in His Spirit and allow Him to be raised up in us.

——— **STEP TEN - ACTION** ———

Step Ten is a maintenance step. In Steps One through Three you made peace with God; in Four through Seven, you made peace with yourself; in Eight and Nine, you made peace with others. Now, in this step and in Step Eleven, you will be doing what's necessary to maintain that peace with God, yourself, and others.

Meditate on this step before going on:

**Continued to take personal inventory and
when we were wrong promptly admitted it.**

You will continue to take ongoing and daily personal inventories so you can keep your house clean and your relationships in order. Periodically, you will want to take a formal, in-depth inventory, beginning at that point where you finished the last one in Step Four. To do this, return to Step Four and follow the instructions given there.

The purpose of the Action below is to give you an overall look at where you've been and where you are now.

A. *Taking Action*

Personal Profile:

As you have progressed through these steps, you have discovered many things about yourself. This knowledge keeps you out of denial and in reality, thus helping you to maintain your peace with God, yourself, and with others.

The following suggested listings summarize the various aspects of your personality as you have come to better understand yourself. Simply list the things you have learned about yourself as you have taken these steps. Add to these lists daily as you learn new things.

   1. Assets:

   2. Defects:

   3. Liabilities:

   4. Resentments:

5. Fears:

6. Addictions:

7. Patterns:

8. Habits:

9. Tendencies:

10. Moods:

11. Spiritual Gifts:

12. Special Talents/Abilities:

13. Hobbies:

B. *In your journal:*
    1. What changes have you experienced today in your thoughts, feelings, or behaviors as the result of taking these steps?
    2. In what ways have you discovered God or sensed His presence in your life?
    3. What victories have you had?
    4. What defeats have you had?

STEP ELEVEN

**Sought through prayer and meditation
to improve our conscious contact with God as we understood Him,
praying only for the knowledge of His will for us
and the power to carry that out.**

Steps Ten and Eleven are the maintenance or growth steps. As I've said, Step Ten throws us back through Steps Four through Nine and adds Step Twelve. Now we'll find that Step Eleven throws us back into Steps One, Two, and Three.

In Step Three we made a decision to turn our will and our lives over to the care of God as we understood Him. As we grow in our conscious contact with God, He begins to unfold in our lives and we begin to grow in our understanding of Him. We walk out that third step decision here in Step Eleven.

Peace with God

In the overview we said that Steps One, Two, and Three gave us peace with God. In Steps Four through Nine we made peace with ourselves and with others. In Steps Ten and Eleven we maintain that peace. In Step Ten we're maintaining the peace with ourselves and others, and in Step Eleven we're maintaining and improving on the peace that we've made with God, or the relationship that we have with God.

The product of that peace that we achieve is a deeper, more meaningful relationship with God as we grow in our understanding of Him and as His life begins to well up in us.

Prayer and meditation

Let's look at prayer and meditation first. Prayer is talking to God. Meditation is listening to God.

In prayer and meditation, on a daily basis, we admit that we're still powerless (Step One); and we have to choose a power by which we can live and we decide that that power is going to be God (Step Two); and we actively choose that power and ask God to take care of us, run our lives, keep us from our compulsions, keep us from our addictions (Step Three); and we pray for the knowledge of His will for us and the power to carry it out.

I recommend that you pray and meditate in the mornings and in the evenings—but especially in the mornings.

The Committee

There's a committee whose goal and purpose is my destruction. I used to wake up every morning to a voice in my head. It was the Chairman of the Committee. He was always waiting on me. He would notify me that the Committee had been meeting all night on my behalf and that they had come to some conclusions. He would inform me that most of what I had done all my life was a failure and that, indeed, I was worthless. He would go on to tell me that I might as well not bother to get up because I would just continue to make a miserable mess of everything.

Then he would say things like, "Do you feel the small pain down in your ankle? That's bone cancer. By noon today it will have progressed up to your knee, then into the groin, and by midnight it will be all the way to your brain. You'll probably be dead by tomorrow morning, so there's really no sense in getting out of bed. Just go ahead, roll over, pull the covers over your head, and try to escape back into sleep, because the only thing that's going to be in store for you today is misery and more of the same drudgery. Besides, you can't do anything right. You never have. Just stay in bed and die...unless you want to get up and drink..."

Sometimes I'd hear all the Committee members talking at the same time—the judge, the martyr, the egomaniac with the inferiority complex, the addict, the justifier, the critic, the defender, the controller/manipulator, the guilt-provoker, and Mr. Mad. They can never agree on anything and they can never come to any conclusions except one: that I don't deserve to live.

I've learned to tell them to shut up. I've learned to go to God.

So, for me, it's mandatory that I begin to focus on the first three steps as early as possible upon my awakening, and I have to pray and meditate to get started on the right track.

My time in prayer and meditation

In the mornings, the first thing I do is read scriptures. I read something from the Old Testament and something from the New Testament, and usually some Proverbs to see if I can gain some kind of wisdom to keep from shooting myself in the foot that day.

Then I pray, on my knees. I use an outline for prayer called ACTS, just for the sake of keeping me in line. It's easy to remember. It's a little acronym that breaks down like this:

> A for adoration
> C for confession and forgiveness
> T for thanksgiving
> S for supplication.

So, I begin with some worship and praise (adoration). You can do this however you choose to do it in your prayer time.

Then I move to confession and forgiveness. This is the part where I acknowledge that I might have a defect or two left. I confess my sins, my faults, and ask forgiveness for myself. The forgiveness of others is very important. We need to forgive whomever we've taken up an offense against. We need to let go of whatever stumbling blocks or offenses that we may have picked up yesterday or that we've been holding on to. Be forgiving. There are some people that we can't forgive for more than five or ten minutes at a time, but just start somewhere, and see if you can build on it.

Then I go to thanksgiving. I list my blessings and thank God for whatever I need to thank Him for.

And then supplication. That's prayer for others—intercession—and prayer requests for myself, too.

After I finish the prayers, I usually meditate—that is, I do some listening—listening to God. During this time I use something called contemplative prayer.

Here's how it's done: Let your body relax, and let all the tension and all the thoughts go out, and all the preoccupations. Either meditate on a small scripture or meditate on just one or two words. I meditate on Jesus, the Holy Spirit, or Abba Father[1]. I just think about God and try for a while in the contemplative prayer to love God. It's quite an exercise. It's pretty interesting to try to do this. Just spend fifteen minutes if you can, or at least five minutes, just trying to love God. It's quite rewarding.

So I use the contemplative prayer for meditation time. I don't cross my legs and get in the yoga position, "om," or any of that kind of thing. I have something from the Word to meditate on.[2] And God will give you, or He gives me, the meditation of my heart. My mind will wander now and then, but I just return to my beginning meditation and try to love God.

This is my daily routine. If I don't do this, the Committee will rule my morning and my day.

So, pray and meditate in the morning.

Now in the evening, as I talked about in Step Ten, we need to reflect on the day in prayer. We need to close out the day and take inventory for the day. If we've harmed anybody, we need to see about making amends to

---

[1]Romans 8:15

[2]"My meditation of Him shall be sweet: I will be glad in the Lord," Psalm 104:34.

them. If we've done pretty good through the day, we need to give ourselves a little pat on the back and say that we're making progress. Take a reading on ourselves throughout the day, and thank God for the day, and try not to go to bed with any anger or offenses on our hearts. If we need to forgive somebody or let something go before we go to sleep, we need to do that. There's a scripture that says, "Don't let the sun set on your anger."[3] And we need to do that. Let those things go in the evening.

So those are the times and some suggested methods for prayer and meditation.

To improve our conscious contact with God

The step says we're seeking to "improve our conscious contact with God." That's different than just being aware of God's presence or existence. Having a conscious *contact* with Him goes beyond *being aware* that He exists. Hopefully, adding the process of these steps to our salvation experience will deepen our relationship with God.

If I'm going to have a relationship with somebody, I have to spend some time with him. You don't have a relationship with someone by just meeting them one time and saying, "Hi, there. I'd really like to get to know you. I'd like to have a relationship with you. Have your machine call my machine and leave some messages. Let's do lunch sometime." That's what we do a lot with God. We run in and get our quick fix—we get born again, go to church, sit under the Word, and we have someone outside of ourselves do for us what we're not doing for ourselves in our relationship with God.

We say, "You tell me about God. Let me just sit here and receive this. Oh, that was great. What a great sermon. That was really edifying. Thank you very much. Now, I've got to go sell refrigerators," or whatever it is we do. And, "Yeah, I prayed this morning about three or four minutes while I was shaving. I had a real moment with God there. He and I are getting closer all the time."

If you're going to have a relationship with someone, you have to work on it. If you're married, you know what I'm talking about. You don't get married to your wife or husband and say, "Well, the courtship and the romance is over and I've hooked 'em and they're tied in, so now I can just go fishing and put the relationship on automatic pilot." It won't work. You may even be divorced because it didn't work.

A relationship with anyone requires paying attention to it, and it requires time and involvement. That's what the eleventh step is about.

If I turn my will and my life over to God for Him to run my life, then I need to spend some time with Him to find out how he wants to run it. I need to be involved in prayer and meditation and some specific activities

---

[3]Ephesians 4:26

that involve Him and *how He says He works* in my life. Not how *I think He ought to work* in my life.

I spent most of my early years deciding how God ought to work in my life and then telling Him, "This is how You ought to work in my life." Then when He didn't work that way, I'd go back to Him and tell Him how mad I was at Him about not working in my life the way that I thought He ought to. After I beat myself nearly to death with all that and nothing worked out, I finally decided that I'd read the book that He wrote (the Bible) and find out how *He* says that He works in human beings' lives—how He says He fellowships with us, and how He says He wants to get to know us.

This relationship that I have with God has been improving. It's been getting closer and closer, specifically because of the kinds of activities that I'm talking about here. Not so much because I've *done* something for God, but because I've sat and spent some time with Him.

We're always thinking, or some of us are, that since we have Jesus now, we need to jump up, flex our muscles, and go *do* something for Jesus. Our job is to abide in the vine.[4] There are scriptures that say that He will give the increase—all we have to do is suit up and show up, and He will do the things in our lives and through our lives that He wants done.[5]

So the essence of Step Eleven is increasing our conscious contact with God and having fellowship with God—finding out what His will for us is, and how He's going to work that out. St. Augustine said something about your life being a prayer, just a constant prayer all day long. That would be something that's in line with improving our conscious contact with God—being aware of God all day, in everything.

As we understood Him

Let me briefly repeat what I said in Step Three about "as we understood Him." This does not mean that I get to make up my own god any way that I want him to be and that's the way he'll be. This means "as you come to understand *God*." In other words, the only way you can come to God is "as you understand Him."

Praying only for the knowledge of His will for us and the power to carry that out

Next the step says, "praying only for the knowledge of His will for us and the power to carry that out." That's some really good advice. That's a real *safe* prayer. You can spend all the time you want to praying that and never get in trouble with your prayers. Ever. It'll keep you out of the "bless

---

[4]John 15:4-5
[5]Matthew 6:33; Ephesians 2:10; Hebrews 4:10

my plan" syndrome that we tend to fall into.

"I have a plan, God. Bless my plan. It's a great plan, and I'd like for it to work out like this, and in this time frame. I'd like to have this guy come into my life, and this girl come into my life, and this money come in about two o'clock, and this job," and so on. The eleventh step gets our self-centeredness out of the way and lets God have His way with us.

Someone might say, "But praying only for the knowledge of His will for us is really boring. Besides that, I've got these friends who are in trouble, and I want to pray for them so good things will happen to them. Can I just say, 'If it be Your will?'"

Sure. I've gotten so I pray about everything, all the time. But not so much "bless my plan," but more like "If this is Your will, let me know that, and let's get some doors open and close these," or "If I'm supposed to meet this guy or talk to this person, then make it obvious; and if I'm not, let's move on to where we're supposed to be." That kind of thing.

How much you should expand on "praying only for knowledge of His will for us and the power to carry that out" is directly related to how honest you are with yourself and your motive, and where you are in your recovery or your walk with the Lord.

In my early recovery, I said, "I don't know how to pray."

My sponsor said, "It tells you right here—pray only for the knowledge of His will and the power to carry it out—that's it. You begin with that. Don't worry about anything else right now."

Because it's so easy to pray out of self-centered motives rather than God-centered motives, we can get off into something that's not in God's will or plan for our lives. So, we just begin praying this simple prayer. Then, as we grow in our relationship with Him, we'll grow in the knowledge of His will and His plan for us. As that happens, our prayer life will grow, too.

God's heart

As I've continued in this Twelve Step process, and in prayer and meditation, I seek not only the will of God, but I seek the *heart of God*. For years and years I sought His will, and now I believe He wants me to seek His heart. If I have the heart of God, I'm going to treat you a lot differently than I would treat you in my self-centeredness.

As we move from Step Eleven to Step Twelve, we find out that the great commandment that Jesus gave us is to love the Lord our God with our whole heart, our whole soul, our whole mind, and to love our neighbor as ourselves. I've always had a lot of trouble loving my neighbor as myself, because I tend to be self-centered, self-serving, self-pitying, self-propelled, self-interested—so whatever happens to you is your problem. That's my human nature, and I have to have that nature exchanged for God's nature—that hardened heart exchanged for God's heart. So that's why I'm not only asking for God's will, but asking for God's heart.

This process has made me more sensitive to other people and their needs and their feelings, and it has improved my relationships with other people. As I've said before, my problems are minimal until I enter into a relationship with someone else.

Knowledge of His will

Now, we go to the giant question of Step Eleven.

*How do I know that I am in the will of God—
and how do I know when I'm in self-will?*

The best answer I know of, so far, is to ask myself what I'm doing, how I feel, and am I at peace. If I feel disturbed, or dis-eased about my motives, then there's a very good chance that I am out of the will of the Father.

Now, that doesn't mean that I'm not going to have feelings coming into my life that are negative feelings. I may get angry, or I may get sad, or get depressed while I'm going through the day. But I'm talking about deeper, more abiding, intuitive feelings about a decision that I've made or an activity that I'm involved in—how do I feel in my heart about that? Do I feel at peace?

If it rests in a place of peace with me, then I'm probably in the will of God—I probably sought the heart of God. If I have to force or rationalize that decision or that activity, chances are that it's out of the will of the Father.

Also, if it doesn't line up with the Bible, the word of God, I can be pretty sure I'm missing it.

Another way of discerning God's will is to use the feedback of another mature believer who's involved in these steps.

So, as I'm walking through the day, trying to do my job, I need to examine my motives and practice being honest with myself. If I'm not at peace with the decisions that I'm making, then I probably need to back up. And, as I said, always check it with the Bible, the word of God, and check it with another trusted believer.

As we improve our conscious contact with God through prayer and meditation, our understanding of Him grows. We come to know His heart and His will for us. The more that we spend time with Him and in His word and experience His heart, the more confident we'll become in knowing His will.

Ask, seek, knock

In the Sermon on the Mount, Jesus said: "Ask, and it shall be given you; seek, and you shall find; knock, and it shall be opened unto you: For every one that asks receives; and he that seeks finds; and to him that knocks it shall be opened."[6]

The eleventh step is actually putting that into practice: asking, seeking, and knocking. It's a command of God and it's a responsibility on our part that comes with having a relationship with Him. As we enter into that relationship, He puts a thirst in us to want more of Him instead of more of those other things that we've always wanted.

We ask, seek, and knock through prayer and meditation—by spending time with Him. He tells us to knock on the doors and He'll open them. He doesn't tell us He'll just open the doors because we're standing there. He says, "Knock on the doors," and He tells us to ask and we'll receive.

Doings

After we've been born again we think we've got to go out there and do something for God. But we can't do anything for God. God has to do the doing. We're powerless. Jesus didn't "do something for God." He just sought the relationship with His Father, rested and stayed in that relationship, spent time alone with His Father, and then He just walked around. People would ask Him things and He'd answer questions. They would ask to be healed and He'd say, "Here you go. The Father's healing you."

We need to stay in utter humility, in that position of "He's God and I'm not; He's got the power and I don't; He does the doing, I do the showing up." That's the attitude that we need to have, and we need to stay in a position of asking, seeking, and knocking.

God says, "You have not because you ask not."[7] And we do not ask, because we don't think we deserve. We can't accept who we are in Christ because we don't feel like we deserve to be who we are in Christ. Nevertheless, *we,* in our *own* strength, try to be that person. When we do that, we always fall short. The way to be that person is to seek more of Him, knock on the doors that He's standing behind, and let Him open them.

What do we ask for? We ask for the things that the Father would have us to have—things such as the Father's heart, the Father's wisdom, knowledge of Him and His ways and how He works. And we ask through brokenness and humility, not out of pride and self-righteousness.

Now that doesn't mean that we're going to be passive in our relationship. With the relationship comes a responsibility, but we misunderstand what our responsibility is. The responsibility is not, "I need to go build these buildings, I need to have this TV program, I need to show off for God, or win the universe for God." The responsibility is, "I need to enter deeper and further into the relationship with Him, and then I need to walk out there and enter into relationships with other human beings and love them. God will do the knitting and healing."

---

[6]Matthew 7:7-8
[7]James 4:2

We have a job and it is to ask, seek, and knock—He commands us to do that. His part is "it shall be given you...you shall find...it shall be opened."

Come as children

Jesus said that we can't enter the kingdom of heaven unless we come as little children.[8] Little kids don't come expecting conditions. They don't come with a lot of baggage. They just show up and say, "Give me two dollars." Their attitude is, "You're the dad, I need two dollars, put it in my hand." They don't think about, "Where are you going to get two dollars, Dad?" You're the dad, and dads have two dollars.

The classic line comes from the kid who wants some money and when Dad says, "I don't have it," he says "Well, just write a check." They don't think about how the money gets into the checking account. They assume there's always a blank check. We need to have the attitude of the child as we approach the Father. Especially when it comes to receiving.

God wants to give Himself to us in a relationship. But a lot of us don't believe that. We think we're too insignificant. Or that He's too busy. "I've got an awful headache, but I couldn't ask God to help—He's got bigger things to think about."

God loves us

I believe that God's basic nature is love. I don't think that we can even fathom the depth of what that really means. If love were like a substance that you could hold, that's what God would be. Love is His nature, that's what He's made up of. He's got to have something to love, and something to love Him back.

So, the Father calls us[9] and we become willing to let Him in. We ask Him in. After we ask Him in, there is a responsibility that goes with that relationship, just like it goes with any relationship. We have the responsibility to grow in that relationship. It comes under the heading of ask, seek, and knock. We are commanded to seek Him further; to knock on the doors and He will open them, not us; and we're told that if we need something, we're to ask for it—in prayer. The prayer of a believer penetrates the heavenlies and edifies the Father; and the Bible says that it's the Father's good pleasure to give us the kingdom.[10] So, what fires His rockets is for us to show up and ask for the blank check. But we don't do that, because of our shame, guilt, spiritual and religious baggage. We show up and go, "Mary Lou should have this, but I don't deserve it."

So, our basic responsibility as believers is to ask, seek, and knock. The rest of it is to suit up and show up.

---

[8]Matthew 18:3
[9]John 6:44
[10]Luke 12:32

——— STEP ELEVEN - ACTION ———

In Step Ten we're maintaining the peace with ourselves and others, and in Step Eleven we're maintaining and improving on that peace and on our relationship with God.

Steps Ten and Eleven are the maintenance or growth steps.
Step Ten takes us back through Steps Four through Nine plus Twelve. Now we'll find that Step Eleven throws us back into Steps One, Two, and Three.
In Step Three we made a decision to turn our will and our lives over to the care of God as we understood Him. In Step Eleven we enhance that decision.
So, Step Ten tells us to take Steps Four through Nine; Step Eleven tells us to take Steps One, Two, and Three.
And that's the purpose of this step: to maintain that decision to turn our will and our lives over to the will of God.

Meditate on this step before going on:

**Sought through prayer and meditation
to improve our conscious contact with God as we understood Him,
praying only for the knowledge of His will for us
and the power to carry that out.**

A. *Taking Action*
   Check yourself out:
   1. How have you seen God at work in your life today?

   2. How have your experiences in taking these steps changed your view of God?

   3. Are you becoming more trusting of God in the everyday affairs of your life?

   4. Is this trust causing you to be more at peace with yourself, with God, and with others?

5. What confidences do you have now that you did not have before?

6. Where was your life headed before taking these steps?

7. Where do you think your life is headed now?

8. What major changes have occurred in your life during these steps?

9. How do you think these changes will affect the lives of others in your relationships?

10. What do you now have to give away to others that you did not have before?

B. *In your journal:*
1. What changes have you experienced today in your thoughts, feelings, or behaviors as the result of taking this step?
2. In what ways have you discovered God or sensed His presence in your life?
3. What victories have you had?
4. What defeats have you had?

STEP TWELVE

Having had a spiritual awakening as the result of these steps, we tried to carry this message to others, and to practice these principles in all our affairs.

There are three parts to this step.

(1) It tells us when it's time to take the twelfth step; that is, to use it or apply it.

(2) It tells us to whom we're going to try to carry the message.

(3) It tells us that we need to take the principles that we've learned up to this point and practice them in all our affairs.

Having had a spiritual awakening as the result of these steps

Even when I was drinking and using drugs, I used to have things happen to me—car wrecks and incidents like that—and God would protect me from harm. In early sobriety, I had a lot of special things happen, including just getting sober. Those things that happened were what I call today, "spiritual experiences." In other words, God did some things in my life or protected me from someone or some thing for no apparent reason. And looking back, I can see that God had His hand on me.

In recovery, as I attempted to learn more about myself and learn more about God, I continued to have certain kinds of spiritual experiences, such as "coincidental" meetings with people showing up in my life at the right time or something working out financially—many different experiences.

Step Twelve speaks of an *awakening*, which is different, to me, than an *experience*. It may be an experience, but it's different.

There's an appendix in the back of the Big Book that defines "spiritual experience"[1] and it qualifies some of the things that were said earlier in the

---

[1] *Alcoholics Anonymous*, p. 569.

book, because some of them were radical. It's like some of the things we say in many churches, "Just come on in here and get born again, and God will come into your life, and everything's going to be fine." We may not say it that way, but that's the kind of message that we give—a message which would indicate that we need to come in and have this lightning bolt experience. If we don't have that experience, then we've missed something—we didn't get it.

So what they say in this appendix is that the spiritual experience is a growing kind of thing. We have an initial experience, then we grow in that experience, we learn, we begin to unfold, and God begins to reveal Himself to us.

As we take the Twelve Steps, we come to know ourselves. The more we come to know ourselves—exactly who we are instead of the lies about ourselves—and the more we begin to drop the layers of lies and bondage in ourselves, the more we become who we are in Christ Jesus.

Sometime between Step One and Step Nine, we can expect to have had not just a spiritual experience or a series of experiences with God but an awakening that occurs in our spirit—a spiritual awakening. It's something different than a spiritual experience; it's in addition to a spiritual experience. That awakening is a waking up of the Spirit of God whom we've asked into our hearts. We can tell that there's been a birthing inside of us. We know something's going on. We become more aware of God-kinds of things going on. We become more aware of God Himself. We feel closer to God. Our spirit is *awakened,* in addition to *experiencing* something spiritually.

I didn't know the difference between these two until this awakening happened to me. I always equated spiritual experience and spiritual awakening as the same thing. Then, as a result of becoming a born-again Christian and taking these steps, I got up to Step Nine and experienced a *real* spiritual awakening. The Holy Spirit really awakened and quickened my spirit within me. I was a different person. Believe me, I'm a different person today than I used to be. I'm a different person this year than I was last year, but I'm a *radically* different person than I was before my sobriety.

But it didn't just happen one night. I received the Lord Jesus one night, but my becoming a different person overall and throughout has been a growing set of spiritual experiences through the steps which led to a spiritual awakening.

That's what they're talking about in this first phrase of Step Twelve, "Having had a spiritual awakening as a result of these steps." There's a particular kind of awakening that occurs by taking these steps.

The way that this occurs is: We get God in our life in the first three steps. Then in Steps Four through Nine, we begin to get rid of, drop, or take off the things that we have been but aren't anymore because of Jesus.

(One of the things that's so difficult about Steps Four through Nine is that we're peeling this stuff off that's glued to us, that we've been used to, that we've befriended, that we grew up with. We've been told we're this way, we've learned how to be this way, the pain is comfortable, and now—

we're ripping it off. We're taking it out of there and we're giving it to God and saying, "Get it out of there, and keep it out of there." That's why it's so difficult.)

So, in Steps Four through Nine, we drop the things that we are not and become who we are. We have to be careful not to slip back into the human doing syndrome, into the dysfunctional family rules, the rituals, the religiosity, and all that. We tend to think we have to *earn* something. That's not the way it works. The way it works is that we get rid of what we aren't and automatically become who we are in Christ. This is what repentance does for us.

Then in Steps Ten and Eleven, we maintain who we are by keeping free from the old baggage. When it comes up, with God's help, we keep it off of us. So, by the time we get to Step Twelve, the awakening is becoming who we are in Christ Jesus. I mean, *really* who we are. Walking it out. Being Jesus in the flesh.[2]

We tried to carry this message

I have found that there's also a particular time that we are to do the twelfth step. It tells us that having had a spiritual awakening as the result of these steps, *then* we try to carry this message to others.

The message is our *experience, strength,* and *hope* that we acquire from God through this process. Before we have the spiritual awakening, we don't have this message. We have a different message. Everybody has a message to carry, but until this becomes *your* experience, strength, and hope, and until *you* have a spiritual awakening as a result of this process, you don't have *this message* to carry. You may have information to carry, but you don't have this message.

Let me move over into religion for a moment in order to give you a better understanding of what I mean by that. How effective have you been, or has someone been with you, who hasn't really had the experience of the gospel, who hasn't really had the experience of what the scripture talks about, but has a lot of information about the gospel and about religious things and about God? They've come to you and tried to impart that information to you—or beaten you up with it.

And how well have you done with someone who has said, "Well, I've got this problem..." And you said, "Well, let's get some scriptures. Let me check the concordance, and let me get some things here—and here's some information for you. Here you go. Now take that information and get well. Call me and let me know how it turns out."

This lack of understanding and shallow insight into people heaps

---

[2]Galatians 2:20: "I am crucified with Christ: nevertheless I live; yet not I, but Christ lives in me: and the life which I now live in the flesh I live by the faith of the Son of God, who loved me, and gave himself for me."
Romans 8:29: "For whom he did foreknow, he also did predestinate to be conformed to the image of his Son, that he might be the firstborn among many brethren."

more guilt, shame, and religious abuse upon the person seeking deliverance from their human condition.

The heart of the principle of the Twelve Step program as it came out of the Oxford Movement is this: here's two people who share a common problem, and they throw their arms around each other and say, "You're like me and I'm like you and we've fallen way short of the mark, and we don't have any answers, but it appears that these principles will lead us on a path, and if we do this together, God will intervene in our lives and change us. So, let's do this. We can do this."

The message

It's hard to share your experience, strength, and hope if you haven't had any experience, strength, or hope. So until you have that, you don't have this message to carry. The message you *do* have to carry is your message at whatever point you are. "Well, I've started working on Step One, and I'm still crazy. I still can't stop eating five cream pies in the afternoon. I can't stop going to the discount store and filling up my cart. Can't stop beating my wife (or husband). I can't stop lying. Can't stop this, but this is where I am, and sounds like you're about the same place. Let's get honest with each other and see if God can do something for us."

That's the message that you have. You have hope. "We've got this problem, and there's some hope for folks like you and me. We can stop doing this with God's help. That's what they tell me. I met so-and-so at the Twelve Step meeting, and he said he was just like me. And now he's not."

Even as a Christian, it's okay for things not to be okay in your life. You don't have to be perfect and you don't have to fix everything. Sometimes you may have to say, "I'm glad you thought I was strong, but let me tell you what's going on with me, and how much pain I'm in, and let me tell you what I'm doing with it." And, "If I can do it, you can do it."

(My dad used to say, "If I can make this program, a German shepherd can do it.")

So, *this* message is more than giving out information. You can go to Bible school, or you can buy a bunch of Twelve Step books and read the books and memorize the steps and memorize the information and go beat somebody up with it, but that doesn't mean that you've had the experience of it, and you definitely haven't had the awakening.

The only way I know to get this awakening is to go through repentance. Steps Four through Nine is the actual process of *repentance*. It's totally scriptural. The principles that are set forth in these steps are scriptural, and it's the process of repentance. As I've said before, repentance comes from the Greek word *metanoia* which means to change your thinking. The problem is that we haven't been able to change our thinking. We can pray about it and do this and do that, but we can't change it—or at least I couldn't until I totally surrendered these areas of my life to the Lord Jesus Christ and He began to deal with them and give me victory over them.

I wanted to change my thinking. I could read about some ways to think that were different than the way that I thought, and go try to do that. But until I entered this process of repentance—which is letting go of the lies or letting go of what I'm not, and becoming who I am in Christ Jesus, and letting God change my mind, change my heart, renew my mind and renew my spirit—I couldn't ever get it done.

We receive and perpetuate religious abuse by having been pounded by religiosity and then trying to pound religiosity into somebody else's head. Someone who's hurting can always tell if you're preaching to them or sharing with them. There's a big difference between preaching and sharing. Preaching has its place when God has appointed it, but sharing yourself with another will almost always open a door for the Holy Spirit to do His work.

So, don't carry the message that you don't have. Carry the message that you do have. Stay in your own experience and your own message, because that's where the power of God is. That's where God meets all of us. He doesn't meet any of us where we're going to be, or where we used to be. He meets us where we are. And He'll meet the person you're talking to where they are and where you are.

We tried to carry this message *to others*

The others that we try to carry this message to is anybody, really, but it's usually people that we recognize as being like us—folks that are in the same stew that we've been in.

As you've gone through this process and you've come to know more about yourself, I'm sure you've noticed that you're able to walk around and meet people and look at them and think, "Oh, I see. It's obvious that this guy came from a dysfunctional family and his father abused the daylights out of him, and he's got the same kind of stuff I've got. I can tell by the way he's talking and what he's doing and how he's a performance-oriented workaholic, just like me."

So, we recognize, or begin to recognize ourselves in others. That's where the scripture in the Sermon on the Mount about not trying to get the speck out of somebody else's eye until you get the log out of your own eye[3] comes in. The work that we do getting that log out gives us the insight into other people who have the same logs in their eyes. That's the way it works.

So we begin to recognize other people who are like us (or like we've been), whether they're food addicts, work addicts, religious addicts, abused people, bound up, hurting, alcoholics—we begin to see that.

As we begin to see these things in others, how do we carry the message? Well, we run down, get our Bible, run out and grab 'em by the throat, get them in a headlock, and then we begin to pound them severely about the head and face and shoulders with the Word.

Or we'll double-book them—get their heads in the middle of two

---

[3]Matthew 7:3-5

Bibles—smash!—beat their brains in—

"Get it? Got it yet? Huh? Didn't hear that, huh?"—bash!

"Get another page! What's the matter with you?"—slap!

No, no, no. Slamming heads doesn't work. It didn't work on me. It probably didn't work on you either. Why do we think it's going to work on somebody else?

We're going to say things like this: "I really understand where you're coming from. Same kind of thing has happened to me. I know what you're talking about. I have a real empathy for you. But there were some things I did that helped me to get over some of the stuff that you're doing and the things that are happening to you in your life now. If you're willing, I'd be happy to share what they are."

The main way people are going to come into our lives is by **attraction**. One of the best ways to get other people in this process is for you to take these steps, have this experience and this spiritual awakening, and people that have known you before will see you now and they'll come to you and say, "You know, I'd like to know what happened to you. Three months ago you were an unhappy, bound-up person. And now you're different, free. What happened to you? Something's happened— you're just not the same way you were."

And that gives us an opportunity to share our experience, strength, and hope. "This is how it was for me—this is the experience of what happened to me in my recovery. This is how I gained strength, and there's hope for you. I didn't think there was any hope for me, but now I know there is, and there's hope for you, too." That's what we share. That's the spiritual essence of what we share after someone has been attracted to us.

It's real strange how God will begin to place people in front of us—people who need and are ready to hear the message. We don't have to go out and stand in the mall with a little Twelve Step sign and work to attract people. It just begins to happen. When this experience and awakening happens in our lives, it becomes relevant to other people. God knows that and puts them in our lives.

A testimony

A lady in one of my lecture sessions gave this testimony:

> I'd like to say that I'm kind of like Paul in that situation where he says I am the chiefest of sinners. In my life I have been the chiefest. I've been a religious abuser. I've been very codependent, because I've had such low self-esteem, and it gives you an ego-high when you are able, by God's word, to say something will happen; but a lot of times you will do that when there are dead men's bones inside of yourself.
>
> I thank the Lord for these Twelve Steps. I have been in denial in my Christian life, and the Lord just shined the light into that

darkness. I still feel like I am a mess, but there are areas in which I am seeing some victory. I've even had to go to my children and say, "I have brow-beaten you with this Bible, and I wasn't even able to handle my own situations." I had to say to my daughter, "Honey, I'm just sorry that I beat you like I beat you with this Word, because you cannot walk where I'm trying to teach you to walk until you have this awakening to do that."

I have carried this religious abuse for many, many years, and did not realize that I was in error. It's exhausting. I'm telling you, I couldn't get it off of my mind. It was like I didn't know who I was—I was tired, I was worn out, and why didn't I just go on and die and get out of this mess? You work so hard and you just get tired. Well, I'm trying to get over being tired. Praise the Lord, I'm being healed.

What a great testimony! There are times when you need to let the Holy Ghost do the work of God and you go fishing.

Jesus said that the Pharisees were wrong in what they were doing. There wasn't anything wrong with the Old Testament laws that they were trying to adhere to. (Though the ones they added on were a bit much, I think.) It wasn't that they were *doing* anything physically wrong, it was the spirit from which they were coming. They had *no* awakening. They weren't awakened to anything. It was all works. It was all human doing. And they would stand up there with a haughty eye and beat up everybody that wasn't *doing* it the way they thought they should. That just creates some more shame. Let's heap some more shame and guilt on everybody.

Practice these principles in all our affairs

What does it mean to "practice these principles in all our affairs"? It means exactly what it says.

We came through the first nine steps to learn how to take the steps and get the deliverance that we've gotten. We continue to take the steps in Steps Ten and Eleven, and then we keep on taking the steps in Step Twelve. So, we take the steps so that we can learn how to take the steps, so we can take the steps and keep taking the steps.

These principles work in *all* of our affairs, because all of our affairs that cause us any problems have to do with relationships with persons, places, and things. Either relationships with a spouse, a boyfriend or girlfriend, a boss, employees, a company, or whatever—that's where our problems come about. These principles, when practiced in all of our affairs, keep those relationships cleared, open, and free of resentments.

And how do we practice these principles? That's what we've been talking about in Steps Ten and Eleven.

Every day we take the first three steps from Step Eleven. "I can't, He can, I think I'll let Him." We're going to turn it over.

Throughout the day we work on Steps Four through Nine. When things arise that get in the way—a relationship, anger, resentment, greed, lust, sloth, whatever it is—we recognize that and we repent of it, immediately. If we've harmed anyone, we make amends to them. Right then or as soon as possible. It's at this point, remember, that we decide whether we're going to be right or be happy. "Am I going to be right, or am I going to be happy?" When you're at peace, you can be both.

In the early years of my sobriety, I would rather have been right. And that's self-righteousness, or self-righteous indignation. If you get over into the religious side, it's self-righteous religiosity.

So, "to practice these principles in all our affairs" is all about using these principles in all of our affairs all the time. All the principles are scriptural. The walk that we can have in our life by utilizing them is the walk that Jesus talks about in the New Testament in telling us to be Jesus in the flesh.

Here was a man who did everything the opposite of the way that all the leaders in the temple were doing things. They hated Jesus. He would go right down in there with the publicans and the sinners and the prostitutes; he'd sit down and say, "I hear you. I hear you, man. This is rough. You know you don't have to do this."

A turning point in my sobriety was hearing a guy say, "You don't have to drink any more." It was one of the most incredible revelations that I had heard. (I can't remember much of the first year I was sober. It was just a fog. My brain was pretty fried.)

I went to the guy and said, "I need to talk to you. Are you sure? Tell me that again."

He said, "I'm telling you, you don't have to drink anymore—ever again."

I said, "Thank you." I could hardly believe it. That comment gave me a release. I thought I had to drink right, but I could never get it quite right. But this guy's telling me, "No, you don't have to do that." Hah—what a revelation! (That's how far gone we can get.)

Whatever your deal is, when somebody comes up and says, "Do you know you don't have to do that anymore?" you become very interested in how to get relief.

And that's basically what Jesus was saying to us. "Do you know you don't have to do this anymore?"

A minister who went through the Twelve Steps discovered he had been a failure at ministry. He really got excited over it. He said, "You mean I don't have to do this anymore?"

So, it's important to practice these principles in all our affairs all of the time. The more these principles are working in our lives, the more others will be attracted to us and the more we'll be in a good place to help them come around.

The principles of the whole Twelve Steps boil down to this:
TRUST GOD
CLEAN HOUSE
HELP OTHERS
on an ongoing basis, everyday.

No turning back

A lady who went through the Twelve Step process said, "I've come too far to go back."

This deal is not easy, and sometimes things get even worse, and you can't go back. You can't go back to the head-in-the-sand mentality or the false Sunday morning smile. "Everything's just fine, I'm just a born-again Christian—oh, it's just wonderful. I'm fine, perfect. Hadn't sinned in years."

I thought I had paid dues back in my addiction. The real dues came later as I grew up spiritually and became an adult. Responsibility was something that I had never wanted anything to do with. Even yet, at times, I'd rather someone else take care of all the responsibility. Growing up and going through the peeling off of the flesh and the dying to self and God getting His hands on me and getting me into position has been real painful at times.

But I praise God for it—and now I can't go back. The ground that I've had to claw my way through is real precious to me. Real precious.

This disease killed my father and it killed my mother. My father was an alcoholic and my mother was a codependent. And if you don't think codependence can kill you, just keep at it. It will kill you. Your heart will stop. Your respiratory system will shut down. It will stress you to the point that it will put you in your grave. My poor mother was still taking care of people on her deathbed. She was trying to give them some of this and fix that. I said, "It's enough. This is enough. You get to die in peace. Let's pay attention to you. You just think about you." So even codependency will kill you—or shorten your years.

My life is not perfect and my children are not perfect, but I try to practice these principles in all my affairs and turn it over to God on a daily basis.

Maybe you are at the twelfth step and maybe you have had a spiritual awakening—but the problems in life don't go away. They may change a little bit, but they don't go away. What has to change is our reactions to those problems. I don't react to those problems the way I used to—I don't react in some self-destructive way. God has set me free.

We've come too far together to go back, haven't we?

John 6:67-68: Then said Jesus to the twelve, "Will you also go away?" Then Simon Peter answered Him, "Lord, to whom shall we go? You have the words of eternal life."

APPENDICES

Appendix 1: SPONSORS

CHOOSING A SPONSOR

You should select a special, supportive person for a sponsor, if available. A sponsor is someone who would be available to you outside of meetings for those times when you need someone to talk to—someone to give you feedback, someone to keep you in balance, someone to minister the life of Jesus to you.

Here are some criteria for choosing that person:

Someone in whom you have trust and confidence.

Someone to whom you can present yourself accountable throughout the process of taking these steps (and maybe longer).

Someone who can speak freely to you about the things they see in your life—holding you accountable.

Someone to whom you will give permission to encourage you in your spiritual journey: to see that you keep moving through the steps, attend group meetings, stay in reality, and be honest with yourself.

Someone who is willing to be there to listen to you and generally be Jesus in the flesh for you during this period of time.

Someone you can call on when you feel you might be losing it, or need to air out your feelings, or need a sounding board to check things out.

Someone who has already gone through the steps or is going through them and has some understanding of the process.

Someone who has gone through the same kinds of things that you expect to be dealing with, if possible.

Someone who is of the same sex as yourself.

If you cannot find anyone who meets all of these qualifications, select someone who meets as many as possible.

BEING A SPONSOR

Purpose:

To minister the life of Jesus to another recovering person.

Qualifications:

To have an empathic understanding of the recovering person. This implies that you are most likely recovering yourself in that particular disease.

To have successfully worked the Twelve Steps and found your life changed by the process, and thereby able to utilize the Twelve Step principles in ministering to the recovering person.

To be willing and available as a sounding board to that person on a twenty-four hour basis.

No formal education, training, or certification is necessary.

Obviously, the more knowledgeable you are of the Twelve Steps and of the issues involved in codependency, dysfunctional families, addictions, and compulsive behaviors, the more able you will be to help others. But start with where you are and what you know. You do not have to be an expert in these areas.

Responsibilities:

Being there. More than anything the value of a sponsor is simply "being there" for that other person. It isn't so much what you "do" as in who you "are." "Being" is more significant than "doing." Whenever that other person is facing a crisis, they are under severe mental, emotional, spiritual, and sometimes even physical attack. They are unable to sustain themselves. They are powerless and need the helping hand of a friend to actively be there.

Listening. The primary need for being there is to be a good listener. To be a good listener suggests that the other person needs to do most of the talking. You often have to resist giving out what seems to you to be the obvious solution. It doesn't become obvious to that other person until he has worked through whatever things are going on inside of him.

Interpreting. As a good listener, you can feed back to that person what you hear him saying about himself. In so doing, you will help him to come to terms with reality.

Praying. At the beginning of every encounter with that other person, it is beneficial to silently pray for wisdom, knowledge, understanding, and discernment. Then, believe you have it. Trust what comes to you. At the appropriate time, speak that word of wisdom, knowledge—whatever you have. Speak it in faith. More often than not you'll find it to be exactly what that other person needs to hear. It will be God's word of truth. "You shall know the truth and the truth shall make you free."[1]

---

[1]John 8:32

Praying over that person. As you progress through the crisis time with that other person, be sensitive to the Holy Spirit's leading when it is time to pray *over* that person.

Praying *over* a person is different than praying *for* a person. You will want to always lift that person up before God in your private prayer times. But when you are face to face with that person, you may find appropriate times to pray aloud over that person. There are no formulated words to pray. The best advice, again, is to ask the Lord to lead you in your praying. Pray what you think you know to pray and trust that.

Checking on the person. Sometimes it is needful for the sponsor to take the initiative to call that other person to see how he is doing. Let him know you are thinking about him and that he is important enough for you to give him a call, write a note, or whatever seems appropriate.

Holding the person accountable. What most people need is that caring listener to simply be there. But we are crises-prone human beings. There are times when the recovering person's will and disciplines weaken and he grows lax in paying attention to those things that benefit him. The sponsor may have to strongly encourage that person to go to Step meetings, work the Steps—whatever! You will learn what is in the best interest of that person.

Being honest. A significant part of reality is honesty. Sometimes honesty hurts, but it is always therapeutic. We sometimes have to love that other person enough to tell him the truth.

Discipling. In the long haul, the sponsor is actually to disciple the recovering person to a place of wellness, responsibility, and on to the twelfth step where he can begin to "give it away" and become a sponsor also.

Intervening. Sometimes in the midst of denial and crisis, the sponsor and other caring family and friends have to intervene on behalf of the diseased person in order to stop him in his destructive path. This radical action requires professional consultation.

Breaking codependency. You must learn how to relate to the recovering person in honesty and reality and not allow that relationship to become codependent. The goal of every codependent should be to learn healthy independence until he can choose to become interdependent.

Ministering peace. Your ultimate goal is to guide the recovering person to peace and serenity with God, himself, and all others; and to the wholeness that will enable him to maintain that peace on a daily basis, and then to give that peace away.

CHARACTERISTICS OF THE CODEPENDENT

We have an overdeveloped sense of responsibility and it is easier for us to be concerned with others rather than ourselves. This in turn has enabled us not to look too closely at our faults.

We "stuff" our feelings from our traumatic childhoods and have lost the ability to feel or express our feelings because it hurts too much.

We are isolated from and afraid of people and authority figures.

We have become addicted to approval and/or excitement (crisis) and have lost our identity in the process.

We are frightened by angry people and any personal criticism.

We live from the viewpoint of victims and are attracted by that weakness in our love and friendship relationships.

We judge ourselves harshly and have a low sense of self-esteem.

We are dependent personalities who are terrified of abandonment. We will do anything to hold on to a relationship in order not to experience painful abandonment feelings which we received from living with people who were never there emotionally for us.

We experience guilt feelings when we stand up for ourselves instead of giving in to others.

We confuse love and pity and tend to "love" people we can pity and rescue.

We are reactors in life rather than actors.

We have either become chemically dependent, compulsive under- or over-eaters, etc.; married one or both; or found another compulsive personality, such as a workaholic, to fulfill our compulsive needs.

WHAT IS CO-DEPENDENCE?[2]

These patterns and characteristics are offered as a tool to aid in self-evaluation. They may be particularly helpful to newcomers as they begin to understand codependence and may aid those who have been in recovery a while in determining what traits still need attention and transformation.

Denial patterns

I have difficulty identifying what I am feeling.
I minimize, alter, or deny how I truly feel.
I perceive myself as completely unselfish and dedicated to the well-being of others.

Low self-esteem patterns

I have difficulty making decisions.
I judge everything I think, say, or do harshly, as never "good enough."
I am embarrassed to receive recognition and praise or gifts.
I do not ask others to meet my needs or desires.
I value others' approval of my thinking, feelings, and behaviors over my own.
I do not perceive myself as a lovable or worthwhile person.

Compliance patterns

I compromise my own values and integrity to avoid rejection or others' anger.
I am very sensitive to how others are feeling and feel the *same*.
I am extremely loyal, remaining in harmful situations too long.
I value others' opinions and feelings more than my own and am often afraid to express differing opinions and feelings of my own.
I put aside my own interests and hobbies in order to do what others want.
I accept sex when I want love.

Control patterns

I believe most other people are incapable of taking care of themselves.
I attempt to convince others of what they "should" think and how they "truly" feel.
I become resentful when others will not let me help them.
I freely offer others advice and directions without being asked.
I lavish gifts and favors on those I care about.
I use sex to gain approval and acceptance.
I have to be "needed" in order to have a relationship with others.

---

[2]Reprinted by permission of Co-Dependents Anonymous, P. O. Box 33577, Phoenix, AZ 85067-3577, (602) 277-7991.

Appendix 3: FAMILY EMOTIONAL STAGES

FAMILY EMOTIONAL STAGES[3]

The way in which a family reacts to the loss of a member (whether it is by death or chemical abuse) moves through stages if it is ever to get resolved. People are not always aware of these stages as they progress from Stage One (Denial) to Stage Five (Acceptance). Stages may be skipped, and it is possible to revert back to a former stage. Your understanding of these stages may help you reach the last stage of dealing with the problem.

Stage One - Denial
It is our tendency to overlook things that are painful. We usually rationalize the problem by saying, "It is just a phase," or we minimize it by saying, "It isn't too bad." A realistic look at the loss is essential to go beyond this stage.

Stage Two - Anger
"Why are they doing this to me?" or "I don't deserve this," are examples of anger. At the heart of this feeling are shame and a feeling of inadequacy. Realizing that the choice to use does not belong to us but to the person who is offending will help us realize that anger does little good for either party.

Stage Three - Bargaining
When we cannot control the choice of the offender, we try to bargain with him/her or with a power we feel can make a change. This effort is usually unsuccessful and may lead back to anger or forward to the next stage. This is another method of attempting control. We must realize that we do not have the power or the responsibility to control another person's choice. This realization may result in a feeling of helplessness and depression.

---

[3]Adapted from the five stages of grief described by Elisabeth Kubler-Ross in her book, *On Death and Dying*, (New York: MacMillan Publishing, 1969).

SHARE YOUR EXPERIENCE

We are always encouraged by the testimonies of what God has done through the use of this book. Will you share your experience with us? Please give us the benefit of your insights as well.

Send your story to: Power Life Resources
P. O. Box 110512
Nashville, TN 37222-0512

POWER LIFE RESOURCES

Boundary Power
How I Treat You, How I Let You Treat Me, How I Treat Myself

by Mike O'Neil and Charles E. Newbold, Jr.

MISTREATED? ABUSED? Then, take charge of your life. Learn how to set healthy boundaries—boundaries that define who you are in relationship to others.

By answering the questions and acting on the information that you learn in each chapter of this book, you can open a whole new way of successfully dealing with life's challenges.

You will learn how boundaries affect you relationally, spiritually, emotionally, physically, and sexually. You will learn the difference between healthy and unhealthy boundaries.

This book will help you identify boundary issues in your life, guide you in establishing new and healthier ones, give you tools to resolve any grief resulting from losses caused by abusive relationships, and close the door to future abuses.

ISBN 0-9633454-2-7   paperback   8 1/2 x 11   181 pages

The Church As a Healing Community
Setting up Shop to Deal with the Pain of Life-Controlling Problems

by Mike O'Neil and Charles E. Newbold, Jr.

The church is to be a healing community to one another. The small support group ministry is one way in which nurtured people can nurture people.

This book tells how to set up small support groups using the *Power to Choose* book. It gives detailed information and instructions for putting a self-perpetuating system in the local church, and it is useful for any Twelve Step ministry.

A portion of the book is educational, addressing subjects such as dysfunctional family life, addictions, and codependency. Other sections detail how to set the system in place, providing helpful resources such as meeting formats and instructions for group facilitation.

Included in the appendices are instructions for presenting an Addictions Sculpt and a Family Sculpt. These portrayals enable participants and audiences to understand the deeper issues behind addictions and the dysfunction caused by addictions and unhealthy family life.

ISBN 0-9633454-1-9   paperback   8 1/2 x 11   187 pages

Power to Choose: Twelve Steps to Wholeness
7 audio-cassettes in album

This audio-cassette series is a live recording of Mike O'Neil as he lectures on the Twelve Steps. They are a concise version of the lectures with some additional insights and include Mike's personal testimony. Those who have read the book will enjoy its freshness as well as those who simply prefer the audio tapes over the reading material.

Power to Choose: Twelve Steps to Wholeness
video-cassette tapes

Small groups working the Steps will enjoy viewing these instructional video tapes together. They are useful for educational purposes in a classroom setting as well. They cover the same material that is in the audio-cassettes. Fourteen sessions on four cassettes.

Power Life Workshops

The Power Life Training Workshops train people how to implement the Power Life Recovery System as described in *The Church As a Healing Community*. The training shows how to put this system to work and explains how it can adequately address the needs of people suffering from codependency, addictions, family of origin issues, religious baggage, relationship conflicts, and more.

This experience prepares one to train others to train others to work this self-perpetuating program. The Workshops include music, drama presentations, lectures, and some "hands-on" Twelve Step experiences.

There Is A Power
Music Album

There is a Power by Ken Soltys is an album of eight praise and recovery songs. Titles are: There's A Power, You Alone, Gospel Groove, Eyes of Love, Crown Him, Pictures, Come and See, and Share the Good News. The excellence of Ken's trumpet skill adds power to his anointed songs. Available on tape or CD.

Presentations

Mike O'Neil's background as a recovering alcoholic; professional musician; experienced Twelve-Step lecturer, clinician, hospital administrator, and consultant; and his dedication to the gospel of Jesus Christ enable him to bring a wealth of experience to the podium. His down-to-earth, humorous style makes his presentations not only educational and inspiring, but entertaining as well.

Dianne O'Neil brings many years of experience to the platform as she orchestrates a live performance of the Family Sculpt. As a recovering codependent, a devoted Christian, trained counselor, and professional musician, Dianne expertly educates and inspires as she gives her message of recovery.

Other dynamic speakers, trainers, and concert artists are available through Power Life Resources for equipping Christians in recovery.

For orders, inquiries, or to contact Mike O'Neil, please write or call.

Power Life Resources
P. O. Box 110512
Nashville, TN 37222-0512

615-331-0691 phone
615-361-0691 fax

from
Voyagers, Inc.
237 Nunley Drive
Nashville, TN 37211

P. O. Box 110512
Nashville, TN 37222-0512
Phone or Fax (615) 331-0691

Order Form

Description	ID code	Single	Prices 2-16 items	18 + items	quantity	amount
Power to Choose, book/Action book	0-9633454-0-0	19.95	17.50	16.50		
Power to Choose, 7 audio-cassette tapes, 14 sessions	PTCA	49.95				
Power to Choose, 4 video tapes, 14 sessions	PTCV	295.00				
The Church As a Healing Community - a manual	0-9633454-2-7	19.95	17.50	16.50		
Boundary Power, a workbook	0-9633454-1-9	19.95	17.50	16.50		
Boundary Power, lectures on 6 audio-cassette tapes	BNDA	49.95				
There Is A Power, by Ken Soltys 　　audio cassette of praise & recovery music	TIAP/T	9.95				
There Is A Power, by Ken Soltys - CD	TIAP/CD	13.95				

Any combination of books may be used for the quantity discount price.　Prices subject to change

Subtotal _____

(if exempt, send copy of exemption certificate) TN residents add 8.25% Sales Tax _____

Shipping/handling, add 10% to Subtotal _____

Charge orders　　　　　　　　　　　　　　　　　　　　Total Amount [_____]

☐ MasterCard　☐ Visa　Expiration Date_____/_____/_____

Credit Card Number

　　　　　Signature_____

Make checks payable to Power Life Resources

Send to:

Name_____ Date: _____

Organization (if applicable)_____

Street_____

City_____ State_____ Zip_____

Contact person_____ Title _____

Phone (____)_____ Fax (____)_____

Please give street address in addition to P. O. Box in order that delivery may be made by a carrier other than the U.S. postal service.

Thank You For Your Order.

98 ptc

Office use only: Date Rec'd	Pd ck #	Date Filled	via